Contents Page

Also Heartily Yours ....

By

Susie Bell

Volume II of Heartily Yours series

Thank you!

I'm a new reader to your blog and I can say from the bottom of my heart that you have saved me from harming myself or worse.

I am now reading all your back posts and for the first time don't feel alone,

Thank you for putting into words every feeling and emotion I have felt over the past few months. ~
Anonymous, Friday, 20th September 2013 from Heartily Mindful Blog

Copyright to Susan Bell

Acknowledgments

The biggest thank you goes to Roger for being my everything, rock, love and support. He has put up with my griping and not doing things immediately so I can continue to write. He has also edited and collated my book including taking the photos for some of my blogs. Roger thank you for putting up with me through the good and the bad times, I love you so much for all you have done and do for me.

I would like to say thank you to all of our friends and family who have heard me ramble on proudly about my book and mental health with all my passion.

Thank you to all those who have helped to let my blog be heard about and continue to spread the word about Heartily Mindful, I am very proud of it especially for Roger who made his first piece this year and will be in the next book.

Thank you to my best friend Julie and her husband Brendon who are a lovely couple. Julie has sat and messaged me for nights on end or sometimes none at all, it will never finish my honorary sister, love you to pieces and always will.

To Paul, Barbara and Julie, what can I say except a big thank you for helping me to realise that work isn't going to always be a bad place for mental health and there are managers that understand. Thank you for the encouragement I have received from you to move on to my next contract and I have now made bigger steps to move on a lot further and do a lot more

Thank you to my Mum and Dad for always standing by me through thick and thin, I love you both very much

Preface

It's now just over a year since I had my breakdown following two years of stress and heartbreak and then pain that led me down a path to a very dark place that I thought I would never escape from. Up until this point I only knew I was not my old self, the words depression or anxiety never crossed my mind until I reached total breaking point, and I had finally sat down with a councillor.

The two years that let led up to this point included the breakdown of my marriage, losing my home, losing my job twice through redundancy, a cancer scare then finally a major back problem with left me in excruciating pain and having to take multiple pain killers.

Of course being a man I couldn't talk to anyone, often sitting on my own crying in the middle of the night with the thoughts I couldn't go on anymore; even before I reached my lowest, darkest point. My family knew I was feeling low; however it was not something that was discussed. After my wife and I had finally split, and just under a year before my breakdown my sister and her husband did try and distract me from my pain as often as possible however the stress of my job was also taking its toll due to long hours, ridiculous expectations and a uncooperative workforce who were also being played by my seniors.

I met Susie just before I reached my lowest point, and I know my path to recovery would have been very different if it wasn't for her support and understanding. It was Susie who encouraged me to talk about how I was feeling, to explain this to the doctor including that on my lowest days I had considered taking my own life. And finally was there as a shoulder to cry on after baring my soul during my counselling sessions.

One thing I have come to appreciate is that for a lot of men it is not the same, the will suffer from stress and depression but keep it to themselves, not wanting to show weakness or appearing to be a failure which of course they are not. As I write this Christmas is looming and I know the feeling I have not being able to provide the level of gifts I would like as I survive on a careers allowance, however for a man with children the pressures are one hundred fold and we it's recognised that the male suicide rate increases during the winter because of this, or the debt it can bring following Christmas.

I am sorry to say that mental health issues are still discussed in hushed voices, even with the amount of media coverage on the subject, and I have certainly come to appreciate the differences between my generation, my parents, and that of my nieces and nephews, and I hope this continues to improve.

Finally there is a saying that pride comes before a fall and I think that is very true when it comes to mental health issues in men, I for one was to proud to tell anyone initially how I felt, I was then too proud to initially ask for help, I was initially to proud to except the anti-depressants which I needed to help start my road to recovery. Now my views have changed and I'm proud to stand up and say I'm Roger Parker I suffered from severe depression, and anxiety and I'm on the road to beating my mental health problems.

I am at present caring for my mum and supporting Susie by editing her books also helping her with her blog when needed. Even though I have finished my counselling and Susie is near the end of hers this doesn't mean that all of the writing will finish or that we will stop because the books are here for others to realise that they are not alone in this dark World especially for those of us who are where we are with in Mental Health. This won't end for either of us, we know though we have friends as that we aren't alone.

Your question is what is the good in Susie writing this? The answer I give you is that she writes to help her get through her days, to help others realise that there is someone like them who are where they are or have been where they are now. She talks to me and other friends for support, she talks to you to help you and to reach out to you, so you know there is someone else.

Why in a book? Because there are people who will not read social media, blogs or other things that I have posted Susie's Poetry.

Read this book and you will feel how other's and myself have by this strong woman, inspiration, encouragement and ways to help yourself out of this by talking.

Susie has not only helped my she has been working through this in and around the stigmatism that we are both fighting against.

Monday, 1st July 2013 - My Brave New World

My New World to some will say keeps starting over and over, perhaps it does, but, it does mean a lot to me:-

You may think about my day
What you think is
What you don't know
You can see the smile painted on
You can see the laughter on the surface

I have put my best foot forward
With my future in my hands
As I walk through the green fields
Hearing the whisper of the wind
And the rushing of the stream

I have been out today
On a walk with my best friend
The one person who is keeping me going
The one person who knows how I am feeling
The one person who has saved me many times

I have had my future in my hands
And he has had his in his hands
What we both saw today
Was something nobody else can see
Something nobody can take away

We put our best feet forward
And watched the Buzzard sawing up above
The Housemartins feeding and nesting
The Swallows flying
And the Little Brown Jobs bobbing around in between

As we watched them up above
We looked at each other in amazement
Looking past the pain in each other's eyes
Watching the pure awe and enjoyment of the birds
And the Damsel Fly

We took the photos we wanted to
To capture the moments and the birds
As we drove to a field with yellow rapeseed and red poppies
To the farmer was pure contamination
To the photographer a pure beauty of nature

As the journey down the country roads
Came to a close
We told each other where I futures lay
Together forever supporting each other
Through life's journey of wonder or pain

I know that today
And every other day I spend like this
Is one of special meaning
Because the wonder and the awe of what is around
The time it took for me to be found

Welcome, today is hopefully a brave new world

Monday, 1st July 2013 - Tick Tock of the Clock

I am literally sat in a quiet room listening to the tick tock of the clock:-

As the clock tick tocks
And the hands sweep past
The seconds
Turn to minutes

As the seconds turn to minutes
And the minutes turn to hours
So the time passes by
All too quickly

As the time passes by
And memories are made
New memories that turn to old ones
And the old ones turn into the past

When the new old memories
Come strolling up
Replace those
With the ones you don't want to remember

So the pain eases out
And the time eases by
Soon you are gathering strength
As history remakes itself with a new path

It will soon be time to be able to replace
The pain with laughter
Laughter you have made in your new life
So listen for the chime

As the seconds turn to minutes
And the minutes turn to hours
You can hear the sweeping of the hands

As the clock resounds tick tock

Tuesday, 2nd July 2013 - The Sooner, The Better

I talked to someone to day who explained that I need to do what I don't do now, going down the dark alley, making a U-turn before I get to far and listening to those around me:-

Turning around
Around from somewhere
You don't want to go
Where you don't feel safe

It's not easy
Stopping yourself
From going down there
Going somewhere you don't want to go

I sometimes feel like
Putting my hands over my ears
Not listening to a word being said
I don't want to hear the words

The words could be
Come back this way
Don't go down there
Take a different path

Stop myself from getting
Agitated at things
From feeding myself with more
More negative feelings

How do I do it
One day I will find out
I will get there
I will stop myself from going the dark way

The sooner the better!!!

Tuesday, 2nd July 2013 - My Peace

This is what I feel my life should be like and will be like:-

I dreamed a dream
Of a World at peace
Where everybody helps each other
When we all talk to one another

I saw a place
A place of hope
One where there is faith
One of belief in oneself

I saw the change
Change in each other
Understanding
A place for support in change

You helped me see this
See what my World could be
Where I will be one day

A Place of peace in my own life

Wednesday, 3rd July 2013 - My New Pathway

You are able to read where I have been tonight and where I am :-

Well, here I am
Sitting and sharing with you
The first piece
From my new room

It is so much smaller
My mind is racing tonight
It isn't sure what to think
How to think

A new friend
A new home
A new house
A new poem

Positive is what I am trying to think
Negative is still running through it
I don't know how to deal with it
This should be an exciting time

I know I will enjoy it
And I am only down the road from my support
I will get there in the long run
No matter how long it takes

The tears will come and go
The smiles will always be there
Painted or real
There will still be me beneath the pain and toughness

The strength will grow
As the rubbish goes
As I start to make an image to help me

Help make my pathway through life

Thursday, 4th July 2013 - If only I could have talked to you my colleagues

I went into work with an extremely low mood and wanting to just go home, please read my post to see what happened:-

Another dark day
One that felt so dull
I didn't think was going to lift
I was trying to think of good things

Good things that were coming up
But, nothing at all got me out of this
The cloud still hung over me
As the minutes ticked faster by

I wanted to shut down
Go home
Go to sleep
I didn't want the day at all

I just wanted the night
So the week would have been
Washed away
Even by the sunshine

My lowness gave me the head
That I didn't need
The tiredness I was not wanting
And the thought about having a duvet day

I started to pick myself up
As I spoke to my other half
Who encouraged me with a few kind words
Words that I really needed to carry on

As the afternoon whiled away
I was starting to feel a little better
Because I knew that I was going home
I was going to roll up in the duvet

Let the black cloud cover me
Just like the duvet was going to
So I could sleep and cry if I wanted
It doesn't matter sometimes what I think

It is just having some kind words of encouragement
Words that I wished I could have asked for
Ones that were needed from someone in work
If only I could have talked to you my colleagues

Friday, 5th July 2013 - This is support!!

Please read about what I have seen for the first time today:

What a busy day
First work
Where I felt stranded
Stranded in the middle of a sea
Sea of people

I needed to get home
But I was late
Home to peace
Home where I know my heart is
Home where my peace is

I have been clouding over today
A day that I was hoping to be good
No-one was hearing me
Nobody listening
Banging my head against a wooden desk

If it wasn't for the fact
That I sat waiting for my car to be cleaned
Taking in the sunshine and being able to relax
I think I would have come home screaming
Screaming blue murder

I have suddenly realised
Why it is being at my partners helps
It is my partner
He is my peace
He is the only one who has a way of calming me and bringing me back

My peace helps to bring me back
Back from my forest of dark
He holds onto my hand
When he hears me screaming
He holds on tight and talks me back to him

Even though I can still feel that cloud
Slowly I am starting to realise what helps me
What brings me back to the shady
Instead of the dark centre
This doesn't help if he isn't there

If it hadn't been for seeing him so early today
I would have or even could have gone back in
Thinking about anyway out of it all
It has taken me a long time to realise what helps
What works, but, it may not always work

It is me who has to keep holding on
It is me who will keep plugging
It is me who will pull and tug
But I know if I turn around even for five minutes
I can see the one thing that keeps me going

The one person who has understood me
The only person who hears what I am saying
He takes me to the edge
He holds me tight with every faith and hope he has

That I will say is love

Saturday, 6th July 2013 - My Darkest Day?

I am explaining what seems to be one of my darkest day and how it feels:-
Feeling somewhat hopeless
And useless
Feel like I am in the way
Want to just put the duvet above my head
And cry

The more I cry the worse I feel
But I can't stop the crying
Because if I do
I know that I will still feel the same
I have felt like this before

I have had too many of these feelings
Too many feelings of wanting
Something to help me
Feel better
For not wanting to cry anymore

My problem is the tears still keep on coming
What would happen if I just walked
Walked out the door
Nobody would be bothered
Everyone is sat outside

As the tears keep rolling
So I keep walking
Down the dark and dingy alley
The alley that seems to have no end
Away from everyone talking about me in quiet corners

To somewhere, where nobody can find me
I want to keep walking
As I hear the mumblings between others
Where I am not in the way anymore
Where everyone doesn't have to understand

When I am stood in the dark alley
It doesn't matter what I do
There is nobody there
It is lonely
It feels like the safest place to be

Yet, I know it isn't
When I look around
All I can see is what is happened
I feel like I don't have to explain my self
That everything I see can be seen by others

I want to shake myself out of it
I want to get into the light
I don't want to be here
But I am
I can't seem to help it

I have no peace
No calm
My thoughts are just running away with me
So I need to stop

I am crying for my angels to hear me, but, they can't

Sunday, 7th July 2013 - Stand By A Man(A piece not a poem)

I don't think there is much I need to say to this except stand by a man:-

A man or mouse?

A whimp or hero?

Do you know how this destroys you, perhaps you should think how it could destroy him?

Even how it destroys your relationship?

If you are single, there is someone out there who will understand what I am about to say, you are not alone, nor on your own.

I do know how depression destroys a man for one reason I was stood supporting one through the start of mine. Don't think about my depression this is not about me.

A man has such pride that they feel that they are unable to break, that they should be the stronger and better to help carry the family, this man carried his family and the destruction of which his past had caused him to break down to what we know as a mental breakdown, meltdown, depression whatever you want to call it, what the doctors called it was a Mental Breakdown

It took a very long time to realise that he couldn't carry on like this, yes, I have spoken about it before, but, this time in a bit more depth because, you see I feel that male depression is taken too lightly (yes, and ours), too differently, we don't see how much we have put them on a pedestal to become the pillar of the family, the backbone we cannot do without, when I'm not saying we can, but, perhaps this is what causes the problem we don't hear what they want to say to us until it is too late and sometimes they just keep struggling until they break.

It takes a lot of strength to realise that there is something wrong, it isn't a weakness, it is a strength because they don't think that they can be ill, that they should keep going. Well hear me now men can fall as well as women, sometimes it is all the harder because they don't know how or when to put their hands up to say I am ill, there is something wrong with me. It took me and his doctor a couple of months of discussion with my partner to say he was ill as well as his back problem.

I had seen it all before in myself. He cried, we talked and he suddenly opened up to me and said that he needed help. I had told him I saw the problems from a while before that and I had been trying to encourage him to find help, he told me that he was glad I understood and that he would speak to the doctor the next time he went back to him in a couple of days. He cried, now, if you have never seen a grown man especially the size of my man(big ex-rugby player) and what was once a bubbly, confident IT Manager you would understand how heartbreaking this was and I ended up in tears for him, with him even.

We knew this was the time he had made the biggest step he had made since the change he made over a year before. He started to go down, with the insecurities of what are you doing with me, are you sure you want to do this? You can go if you want? Everytime he said this I would look a little gobsmacked(the only way I can think to put it sorry) to say the least, I would tell him that I was with him because I could see what was below the pain, not because I felt sorry for how he was. I love him, because I do the same thing now, with him now the tables have turned.

I kept encouraging him that everything was going to be alright, being there for him when he needed me, needed to talk or cry or even rant. I wouldn't just ask him if he was alright daily I would ask how he was, how he was actually feeling even after knowing he had tossed and turned with nightmares.

He went back to the doctors with his back and asked for some help from me by going with him, he was scared, he was like a little child to ask for help, it was hard for me to take him, but I sat in the waiting room as his doctor spoke to him, we talked as we walked to the chemist for his tablets. The doctor gave him a telephone number to call for Let's Talk, a Counselling Service to help him.

He called them the next day, he came down to me and cried, even though he had cried on the phone with the service, he had realised how real all of this was, how bad he had been. The words he was now saying to me were 'I could never have done this without you, you are the one thing that pulls me through not doing anything to take my life, because I know how much I love you and you love me' which made me cry now I can say the tables have turned and I say the same about him.

You see what we don't do often enough is to take the time and spot the real emotional differences is knowing what is right with everything and seeing what is wrong, because we take such a lot for granted. Asking your other half if there is something you are be able to do. I have heard from different places that everyone thinks everything is alright and they are finding it hard to hold it together, when they need to actually fall apart, they need to admit that something is wrong, not for an argument of you are useless or lazy, before you say that stop and think about what you are about to say and see if things are different especially for someone who was funny, active always out and about or doing things.

When you have sat and talked about it, ask him to see someone that it isn't a weakness it is a sign of strength that he has admitted that there is something is wrong, it doesn't matter how minor or on what level it is, he needs to know that there is support around him as I did and encouragement to put it right with counselling or time, it will take time, it has taken time, finally mine has seen the end of the tunnel.

The light has got brighter day by day, the fact he was able to talk to me meant so much, after each counselling session we talk to each other, putting things right with perhaps the little things we need from each other as well as knowing what happened in the past to be able to by the pain inside. I still ask him if he is alright every time I see his mood change, if he seems not his normal self.

What I am trying to say is I think that a man who can step up to a doctor and say there is something wrong, that he needs some help is a hero in my eyes, he is taking the strength inside to step up to the plate so to speak. Don't get me wrong I think it is the same for all of us, but for men it is different in the way that we think that they are invincible and nothing should be wrong with them , we think that they will never fall, but they do.

I have living proof of that from my angel and my hero. I am proud to stand by a man who has been through all of this and that I have seen go through it coming out the other side, he is very nearly there now and I will continue supporting me as he does myself.

I love him very much anyway, but especially for being strong enough to go through a breakdown and come out the otherside.

I stand up with men and breakdowns as I do for any other mental health illnesses, the only thing is the fact I have been through this breakdown with my man. All I can say is try to see the difference before it destroys him or yourself or even both before it is too late, too many relationships are spoilt by destruction of not understanding.

My name is Susan Bell, I am 42 years old I have depression. Today I can stand up and say I supported my partner through his mental health breakdown and am proud to stand by him through thick and thin as he does with me. I will keep on talking until it is heard, until something helps those of us in and around our work/life balance, someone to talk to or understand how we are feeling.

Thank you for listening.

Monday, 8th July 2013 - With Hope & Faith I Will Help

Today sees the light of a new me, a turn around and I hope for good:-

There is someone standing over me
I know there is
To make sure I am alright
Someone who cares
Someone who understands

It doesn't matter if they have
Big white wings
Or if they are just a spirit
From another life
Someone is watching over me

I felt over the past few days
As though they had let go
And then there was a wind
A wind that blew my way

I suddenly felt the warmth
Not just of the summer sun
What I had felt before
As if someone was trying to lift me
Lift me from where I had been

The air had lightened
So had my mood
I knew that there might be a chance
A chance to help me
A chance to be able to help others as I have done

It wasn't just from writing
It for something else
I am determined to get past this
I know how many times
And then I get low

That low period
Is a step back
A step back anyone can take
As long as they see a way forward as well
I am seeing a way forward
I am seeing something

Something I have never done before
Somewhere I have never been
With people who I have never been with
It is scarey
But I know I can and will do

With hope and faith I will help

Tuesday, 9th July 2013 - With Every Step He Has Made It!!

For anyone who loves someone or knows someone who has got over depression or starting to make a difference ask my partner. I hold my head up to call him mine and I would support him again if he needed it. I will always support him in everything:-

Hard work
Courage
Strength
Love and
Care

With the darkest of clouds
Hovering over your head
I know what you have been through
You have never let this get you down
You fought it every step of the way

With the hardest of work
The most determination
I have seen you change
Change to what you should be
Change to you

With the greatest courage
And a little tough love
With some encouragement
You have done what you want to do
You are seeing the light at the end of the tunnel

There have been times
When you thought you would never get through
But you have
You have plucked up so much courage
Through all the tears and the anger

With all of this put With all the determination you have had
And together
I have found you again
You have found you again
Once you have made that final step
I know you will, You will finally have your life back

With all the determination you have had
And got
I know that you are the stronger man for what you have done
You have taken so many steps along the way
Now you stand tall, to say I WAS ILL

This man is the most beautiful man I know
The most amazing man I know
The strongest man I know
For admitting he was ill and that he still is
Even though he so near the end of the tunnel

I am so proud of you
My heart overflows
I love you so much
And I am so proud to call you mine

Keep climbing and the World will be your Oyster

Wednesday, 10th July 2013 - Wanting To Move Forward

I have wanted to move on from where I am today, it took someone last night to help me realise that I am where I am because of my past, I have been rested and taken too many steps back to stop myself from going forward, I have seen my partner move forward nearly at the end, knowing that this will never end completely from his breakdown and for to want to do the same now, he is my shining example a role model if you like, please read:-

I have been looking around today
Working out
Why I am where I am
What I am going to do
I don't want to sit back and let it beat me

I want to fight this
How do I do it
With such a black cloud over me
With a loneliness inside
When I want to live happily

It isn't just the talking
Not just the exercise
Not even thinking positive
It is doing the positive
The positive step by step to get out of the negative

I will get there I know
I am so fed up of being tired
Of always feeling so low
I know that I can and will
Fight all of this

With or without the help
Help from friends
Or even from my colleagues
But I know that from whom I get it
I will be grateful

From those I don't
It is your loss
Because you can't say
I helped you through this
And I can say I did this without you

It is sad to say that
But, oh so true
You know who you're friends are
But also you know
You have fought this fight

That is what it is
A fight
A fight against a hidden illness
One that nobody will see
Until you say something

When you do say it
Wait for the reaction
You will know
Let yourself know
It doesn't matter their reaction

Because you are not alone
There are others like you
You have friends around you
There will be a hand to touch you
A hand to help you

There will always be someone
Someone to talk to you
Who will help you
And support you
There is hope, faith and happiness

Even though you may not feel it now
Somewhere, someone
Is thinking about you
Wanting to support you
Wanting to help you come from under your cloud

I have found a few people
Who want to help me
I am going to take steps forward
I have taken steps back
Now I am going to move forward

Wednesday, 10th July 2013 - I am Who I am

I had the need to write this:-

I am who I am
But, I am not what I am
My name is Susan
Not depression

You may see the sadness
What I want you to do is..
See past that sadness
Look deep inside

Look at the person I really am
The person who lives
Not the illness that is
I am me, Not my illness

Look at me
What do you see?
Do you see illness
Or do you see a human being?

I am a human being
Wanting to live
Living on the edge at the moment

I know and will get from out of my illness!!

Friday, 12th June 2013 - Look in the mirror first!!

(Not a Poem)

Who am I?
What do I look like?

Me, I am a human being, normal looking human being, someone who gets up early to start work at 7am in the morning and does a whole day's work without her colleagues around her knowing what is going on in her mind no matter how low, goes home at 3.30 gets home at 4.30 where everyone knows exactly what I am or who I am.

If you wouldn't know any different than you.
I am not depression. I am not my illness, my illness is not me, I have an illness one that is hidden from people, one that does not show.

There are 1 in 4 of us who at one stage in our lives on many different levels of life have a mental health illness, the mental illness could be a very slight, low level or it could take over our lives(which I will say there is nothing wrong with that).

We all in our everyday lives have to deal with someone who has a mental health illness, just because it doesn't show it doesn't mean we shouldn't understand. The thing about understanding it is comes with respect as well not laughing at it purely because it isn't happening to us and strange things happen to that person.

I look in the mirror each day to dress for work or going out, I want to wear any clothes I want, but I wear dull for some people because that is what I choose to wear. But, I want to put a false smile to be able to show people I am not unwell and I can do my work perfectly well.

I went through an evening only yesterday and a morning today without anyone knowing I am unwell, until I said that I wrote my blog, I wrote to say how my feelings are and that my boyfriend/partner has been through the same thing, because I look no different to those around me.

Why do I have to look different, someone who has diabetes doesn't but, they are still able to say they are ill, someone who has heart problems may not look unwell, but they are still ill, me because I have depression I have to look mad? NO I do not, I don't care what you think I am not crazy, I am having trouble in accepting and coping with situations in my past life.

Why should it be funny someone takes tablets to help them, it isn't, just because you are perfect and can cope with your life doesn't mean others can, we are all different in each and every way which is why our world is so varied. We all have different reasons for being here.

My reason is to live for writing poems and pieces with the feelings that I have. To be told that because I have a mental illness and I should or do look crazy is wrong!!!! I or we are normal

We all judge by the outside so much that we should start looking and thinking about what is really deep inside ourselves and understanding what is around us a little bit more before we judge why people are acting strangely or in a funny way, why they stand back or out in a crowd, or are crying for no reason, why they look sad, have you ever stopped to ask them how they are?

Can I ask the next time you see someone cries that you stop to say hello and see how they are alright?

I would so like someone to ask me how I am instead of are you okay? as a normal everyday salutation. I am a human being like you, next time you look in the mirror, look at me as well

I am no stranger I will put a photo on here and you will see.

I am not crazy, I am not mad and neither are they, we are ill, we have a mental illness, one that can and will be cured, and one that will be shouted out about for as long as I live.

My name is Susan Bell, I am 42 years old, I have depression, I am not depression, I have an illness, I am not my illness, it is hidden, but, now it is out, I don't care who knows or what they know, I am ill and I am getting better. I am a human being, there is no mistake about there, but, most of all I write openly about my illness.

Before you go to bed or after you have read this look in the mirror and see if I look any different, I bet it will say NO!!

Thank you for reading my piece!!

Saturday, 13th July 2013 - Simply The Loneliness Birds

(not a poem)

I don't have to say much more today except read on:-
What do you do?

Do you sit alone?

Is there anyone to talk to?

As a lot you already know I work in an office, it is open plan and a lot of people buzzing around me all day, I may have spoken about this once before briefly in a prose I wrote.

The problem is unless you have someone to talk to there is nothing you can do on a bad day, the day maybe a good one at work, however that doesn't help how you feel, it is the mood that you started from, a thought that has started you feeling this way one which you could shake your head to go to the toilets and cry about, but just won't leave you

This sort of day is so lonely, it isn't until you get to speak to someone who knows and you can cry with them that it finally actually helps and your mood starts to lift in the afternoon.

If there was just one person within the office or even organisation or any company that could just take 5 minutes to have helped at the beginning of the day it would help.

It is the understanding from others of the loneliness this causes and how we deal with it. There will be a moment in your darkness that you say, I hate what this is doing, one day you will find that something turns you around an encouragement.

My encouragement this week was when my partner came home from his last counselling session to tell me that he feels nearly there, he is nearly one hundred percent, that wasn't just the counsellor who said that, it was him, he had fought with strength, determination and everything he had to get to where he is now, he said to me in his own words "There is only one more step to finish and I am getting through that stage already" I could never be so proud of someone.

His loneliness is still there, not as much as it was before. His friends went away, left him alone rather than talking to him, now they realise since we both started to talk about it and going out to their barbecues or evening dinners, that we were missing them as well. The best thing that could have happened to my partner yesterday was a very old best friend got in touch with him and they spoke frankly for a long time on the phone and will keep in touch if there is nothing to add to getting better from your breakdown that was the best present to him. Craig if you ever get to read this thank you so much for that added bonus, you don't know how much it means to him.

It is amazing when you talk about things to people instead of holding it back how things change, how you can be more yourself with help of everyone around you. The monster from the deep has got me and is inside of me, it doesn't matter if it is sunny, I know at the party I am going to I am going to feel lonely in the crowd, I may have to stand in a dark corner somewhere and shed a tear, I know my partner, friends and family who know about my illness will help me as I will also help myself, because to me today this will be the start on the road to my recovery, relaxing, getting to know new people, no matter how scarey, we can all do it is just telling ourselves to get there, I know that seems harsh.

I have struggled with loneliness for such a long time now and meeting some new friends have helped a great deal, to actually talk about my problems rather than sitting under a cloud, I know my cloud has been there as well, but all this and more has helped.

I could never say too much about having friends to be able to talk to about my illness because, it has helped so much to know people are there for you, even the new ones from this weekend.

The last thing I am going to ask is if there are any employers or managers reading this, please could we have some support from someone in the company, just someone to talk to, so that our heads and thoughts can get straight for the day. You never know it may be you who gets it next.

My name is Susan Bell, I am 42 years old, I have made new friends this weekend, I have depression. My partner is still fighting, but, nearly there. I will not stop fighting for the cause for this illness to be heard, it will come out of the darkness as will I and so will some of you.

Thank you for reading

Monday, 15th July 2013 - Step by Step

I have learnt a lot of things over this weekend and one is to be a better person by looking forward and trying to put my life back together, the part that has been destroyed. I have made new friends and I have seen old acquaintances most of all they have understood:-

To sit and listen to someone
To hear them say the words you want to hear
For your heart to skip a beat
As you say that you are ill to someone
For them to say I understand

I understand
Can be a powerful medicine
To someone
That can then be changed to positive
To help someone open up

The hand of understanding
Can be the start of something new
The one part of the puzzle
The one single piece
That is needed to come out of the dark

There are so many things
If you go and ask someone who has been ill
That can turn you around
The first part though is the understanding
Understanding from someone else

Someone who hears what you are saying
They could be in work, school, college, friends or family
It is then that the loneliness starts to lift
Because you finally realise
Realise that you aren't alone, not on your own

In order for us to deal with tomorrow
We have to learn to cope or deal with our past
With someone who is there to understand
To be able to help us through
Step by step

Tuesday, 16th July 2013 - My Stain Glass Window

I have been to where a lot have ladies go every five years to a clinic or doctors to get things done a lot of you will understand when I say how painful this was and my partner could see by the ghostly look on my face read my post and see, it isn't feminine by anyway :-

What to do when the pain hurts so much
So much inside
That you remember back to the first time
The first time you had the pain
That pain that hurt so much inside

You remember the day minute by minute
Hour by hour
And the heat was so hot
As it is now
Yet the pain wouldn't go away

The pain cut through me like a knife
Today it hurt just as much
Especially as it is the same thing being done
But, today
Today was different

Today I had someone with me
Someone by my side
The one person that has helped me
To put the old piece of the past
To rest, realising things aren't the same

As I lie on the bed
with the fan going
The thoughts of my past
Of the day of being left alone
Whilst I lie here, are now becoming dim

I have taken one more step into my future
This won't have to be done again
For another 5 years
But it was worth it
To feel the past pain going away

I want you to realise
Things won't always be the same
The piece of each glass that is in front of you
Will make a beautiful stain glass window
One of which you will have made yourself

As you make that window
Behind it will be a mirror
Of which you will see you,
Growing strong and beautiful
As I am starting to now.

If you remember I took the first step
I said I didn't want to be here anymore
So this pain today is significant
It is different
Because it is with two slightly stronger people

My past has not gone away
I will not forget
I have put it into my stain glass window
Where I can bare to see it with less pain
I love where I am now, but I want to be without my dark cloud

Tuesday, 16th July 2013 - Free To Be Me?

I will feel free to be me without trying to be someone I am not:-
See the sun in my eyes
Feel the wind in my hair
With the rain on my back
And the snow under my feet
I can finally start the weather

The cloud has been above me
For so long
So long, I wouldn't like to say
I have never been able to place things
Not in the right slot of my Window

The pane around the window
Is starting to crack
So that I can place the pieces
Where I want them to go
Not just concealed to a rectangular piece of wood

The freedom I am starting to feel
Will be deep down
It will be within my heart and soul
It will also fight the monster illness inside of me
The one that has been there for so many years

I have taken the first step
I have flown my first fly
I have smiled the first smile
When I am there without the bars around me
I will help anyone at all

One day,
The sun won't blind me
The wind will blow my through my hair
The rain will only fall on my back
I will feel the cold snow under my feet
The Stain glass window will have no wood around it

I will then be free, free to be me

Wednesday, 17th July 2013 - Peace, Hope & Serenity for Me

What I want to give to you is what I have inside myself, peace, hope and serenity :-

You are asking me how I can be
Or How can I be
How can I change
How can I have made that roundabout
With a sorrow in your voice

I have changed
Or turned myself around
Because I suddenly realised
That I no longer want to be here
I couldn't tell you what is going to happen next

I have seen a transformation
Of someone very close
To something ugly
Into a cocoon
Now changed to the beautiful, strong colourful butterfly

It made me realise
Realise that I can aim to try for it
Try to come out of my cocoon too
Instead of being the caterpillar
The caterpillar I have been for over 20 years

For over twenty years I have been
In the hands of control freaks
Abusers, sexual and emotional
I have felt the guilt
The guilt that I should have pulled away

What I have now realised now
Is that I have to put the pieces away
Put them into my mosaic
The mosaic that I started a few months ago
Slowly putting them into a place which I can look at

I will never forget what has happened
I have started to talk
Talk about the things that trigger my memories
So that I don't come into contact with them
One day I will be able to face them without that painful memory

I will be able to face the triggers I hope
With a smile and a new fresh memory
So that I can put that piece away again
So I can look back at it without the pain
I know what has happened, but it won't hurt as much

The old faces that have hurt me
They will just fade into the past
The pain will ease and the picture will be mine
It will not be put together to hurt me
It will be pieced together to soothe me

My angel will slowly unwrap her wings
With each step I take
She will put me down when I am ready
Will let me be when I no longer need her
Watching me each time and each step

It will be like a mum with a baby
Taking tiny steps
Each one will be towards strength
And less pain
I will walk forward to that new life I have made

There is hope, faith and for me to be free!

Thursday, 18th July 2013 – Understanding What You Cannot See

I know the sun is beautiful, hear what I still have to say :

do people judge me
They take one look
And think that things are normal
They hear Mental Health
And think I am mad

Why do you need on see the surface
So shallow
Look beneath the surface
See what is underneath
The hurt and pain
The dark cloud that hovers over me not just the fake smile on top

Sit down and hear what I have to say
Before you tell me what I have to do
I am the only person
Who can help me
All you have to do is hear what I say

I don't need judgement
I need understanding
It is all very well to say Snap out of it
It doesn't work that way
Let me speak, I want you to hear

Sit down
Have a cup of coffee with me
Let me cry
Hold me if you want to
Just let me tell you my story

One day there will be enough understanding
That I will not have to ask any of this
I don't want extra kindness
Just need understanding
Like a diabetic has understanding

Shall I say rather
My illness needs understanding
As we understand, cancer, flu, diabetes & a bad back
We who have it carry it around with us
Hidden, deep inside

If we smile
It is taken that we are well again
Not always
We want to feel normal
Not to be labelled as crazy

We are not crazy
We have an illness
Mental health illness which cannot be seen
One that makes us hurt deep down
There will be a time when we can talk about it to anyone

One day there will be more understanding

Friday, 19th July 2013 - You Are A Hero (not a poem)

What a beautiful day, I just want to pat you all on the back for being a hero and listening to what I have to say, do you have to? No, but, you might as well as you are here:-

A Hero?

A Worker?

A Person who stays at home?

A Celebrity?

All of these have one thing in common as far as I know, we are all human, each one of the above is able to have a mental illness. In my eyes everyone of those above who can talk about a mental illness or admit to having a mental health illness is a hero.

I heard someone recently say that celebrities get a pat on the back and a cheer when they admit to a mental health problem which is great because it does show that everybody can get this thing, this illness that gets everyone down. What we need to hear more about as well are the people who have to go to the office, factory, work in the forces, or anywhere which is counted as a place of work, no don't worry I haven't forgotten those who stay at home because it has become so debilitating to go to work.

I think it is brilliant that celebrities are slowly admitting to what they have and this is not a weakness. As I said before, it is the workers who need to be heard, who need to be helped, for those who have now got to stay at home because there is nothing in the workplace to be able to help them.

Companies are always asking us to be proactive and honest about any disabilities or mental health problems, perhaps it is about time they actively worked towards what they preach and ask from us, to help us with wanting to stay in work, we do not want to go home ill, we don't want to go home because there is nobody to be able to help us, all of us actually want to work. I have applied for a four day week instead of working five days, this can't be done yet, but, it will be done within the next six weeks. This for me is being proactive.

If only employers would have something in place, not just occupational health who will tell you to take time off for a week or two or go and see your doctor. We need someone in work to help us

I know this may be falling on deaf ears, but, I am hoping that there may be one, just one employer who might hear what I say from all of this, how would you feel if you were in the same situation, but this is also to help those who may not be ill yet, but, going down that road and may, may just keep them from going down there.

You do not need to employ someone specifically waiting by the phone, but someone who may be able to do that and do other work, something that can be interrupted for just a few minutes.

I am also talking about for your contract employees that do not fall under the usual permanent staff remit, yes I am one of those and I have been one for 4 years nearly 5 as this current climate will not take me as permanent.

Contract employees or stay at home staff with mental health illnesses need this help as well. Do you realise how many of the staff who resign don't want to tell you it is because of mental health, because they can't work for someone who has no facilities for them to get through their day.

The reason I asked about heroes is that we all for managing to get through the days whatever or however they maybe planned it doesn't matter who we are, we need our illness at whatever level it maybe to be heard, talk about it, to be free enough to talk about it without thinking that we are mad or crazy or having to hide away from it.

Some of us have hidden it or hidden from it for far too long, there is nothing wrong with admitting you have a mental health illness it is a strength not a weakness, something that 1 in 4 of people suffer from somewhere in their lifetime, but this doesn't mean we have to hide it or cower in the corner from it scared of who to ask.

We have brilliant Doctors, nurses and counsellors along with a lot of other Mental Healthcare practitioners who work hard each day and we applaud you for what you do, no in fact praise and thank you for the help that you give us, if it wasn't for this you nor I would be sat reading or writing this blog.

Hold up your hand and ask a doctor for some help, go and see your GP, then you have finally got the strength to get up and do something about it these practitioners who work tirelessly to help us, they are the ones who we need to praise as well as ourselves.

My last note is talk to a friend or a member of your family, someone who will help to support you.

You are a hero, and you need to shout about it, to help the wall to mental health be broken down, because the more we all talk about how we get through this, the more it will help the next person, we may not get a prize, but someone hearing what we say is enough for a hero. - BE A HERO TODAY!!

Friday 19th July 2013 - Rehearsal for Nature

See what I saw today you wouldn't believe I was so excited :-

I have been up with the sun today
Hearing planes from all over the World
They have been flying over head
They have been flying low behind the trees
The sun has glinted on one or two

The birds in the sky all moved out of the way
To watch and hear their metal counterparts
As they sawed against the deep blue yonder
With not a cloud to bother them
As I stood and clicked the button on my camera

Yes, what a day
That was just for practice
Tomorrow and Sunday my adrenaline will pump
As I stand getting excited at the acrobats
Of the mighty metal engineered birds in the sky

As you hear them roar
You want to know if it is all over
You want to see the fumes cover the skies again
Especially of the mighty Red Arrows
After watching Dutch, Jordanian, Italian and our proud Royal Navy up and down.

Round and round
I had to have eyes in the back of my head
At the end of the day came
A beautiful Red Kite and a Sparrow Hawk
What amazing creatures as good as watching the birds from earlier

Wait for the next instalment of whom we see tomorrow
From the back garden

Performance of the Royal International Air Tattoo

Monday, 22nd July 2013 - Thunder Storm

Just about how I am feeling today : -

Can you hear the rumbling?
The rumbling in the sky
Or rumbling in my heart
When will it break
I don't know

The rumbling in my heart is not
A love that is lost
But, being scared of everything
That I was hopeless and have no faith
But I know it is there somewhere

The lift will come soon
The lift of the black clouds that envelope my head
The ones that are inside even when it is sunny
Even when I am having a good time
Worrying if I am doing or saying things wrong

I have had a struggle to keep my mind shut
Shut to the bad things happening
Closed so my mouth doesn't open
Saying the wrong things to upset people
I am sorry that I have

I am upset that I have
Being a hero isn't all it is cracked up to be
It is so difficult to get through
So much to do
It is even harder when I can't say this out loud

Why?
For fear of upsetting anyone
The rain will start outside soon
Hopefully then my rain will start
So it will make it easier to talk

One day I will have sunshine

Monday, 22nd July 2013 - Family

Family Stimatism has to be the worst thing possible when you have a mental health illness, when someone outside the family doesn't understand then there is some understanding and you can help, when the family do not and they turn their back on you it hurts more than ever I know it does:-

Family stigma
What a sad time
A very sad time
When a family in our times can't
Can't support a member in need

They need understanding
Someone has to hold back
Hold back on what has happened in the past
So that their own lives can run smoothly
They cannot sit and hear why, what and when or even whom

For me
I am in the same situation
So ashamed of what has happened in the past
Scared of what is going to be said to me
"Pull your socks up" or "Just think about what you have now"

For me
If I told them half of what has happened to me
They wouldn't believe me
When I left my last husband
They didn't understand

I have friends
Who have now started to understand
Understand what I am going through
I can't talk to my family now
So I am pleased to have the few friends to talk to

I'm not going to tell you get out and find someone
There are a lot of online forums to go
Some who are relaxed and really helpful
I wish I could help more

I can only say to me you are a hero
We need to help our families understand
I know this may not happen
But you never know
The more we all talk about it
We will all understand a lot more

Keep talking to me if you want
I am no professional
I am can only chat back to you or with you
I will sit and hear what you say
Hopefully the wider world will understand.

You Are My Hero for speaking out

Tuesday, 23rd July 2013 - Do You Know?

What do you feel in your heart, do you know who you really are does anyone, what does it mean when we say it, I don't know I have never known, I have only ever shaped myself by what others see me as so that my life can carry on as normal :-

The softness in my heart
That turned so dark
The water in my eyes
Which turned to ice
The bright sun in the sky is fire

It is all so mixed up
I feel so mixed up
I am being told to do this
Told to do that
I am just so confused on who I am

The pain in the softness hurts
More times than others
Some I can put it away
In the ice from my eyes
To let me think about at another time

It isn't easy to do this
To talk about it and say what has happened
But there is something consoling me
Something that helps me
Helps me to focus on what is deep inside

A lot of this is so that I can get through
Through everything I have to change
The change I have to make
For me
To even know who I am

Who am I anyway
Do you know?
Do I know
Does anyone know
Or is it a chance we take on life

A chance that one day
The pain will ease in my heart
Water will fall from my eyes
Not the Ice
Which perhaps has been melted by the sunlight shining not fire

Wednesday, 24th July 2013 –

Happiness is...Taking a look At You

Happiness is... You will probably remember those pictures and sayings, well here is my way of putting what happiness is, please read and if there is anything you want to add comment at the bottom I would be happy to see it:-

Happiness
It is wherever you can find it
When you have a black hole sweeping you
It is whatever you can see it in
When you have the above

Happiness
It is being with friends
Friends who I don't have to explain to
The people whom know where I am
The ones who can see the pain underneath

Happiness
It is sitting and laughing with friends
Ones who can understand
That I could at any moment go low
The smile I have is for the time pasted on

Happiness
Is where I will be one day
All day, every day
It will be time where I will have less pain
From the past problems

Happiness
It is when I will sit hand in hand
On a beach with the sea lapping at my ankles
With the one I am with at the moment
The sun rising, shining and setting

Happiness
Is having finally found where I belong
Where I should be

With someone who wants me for me
Who encourages and supports me in all things
Happiness
Is supporting someone when they need it
Encouraging them in whatever they want to do
Doing new and old things together
Being peaceful with each other

Happiness
Is seeing Mental Health illnesses being understood
Being able to go to work and being honest
For people around you to treat you as normal not crazy
Ultimately the stigma to be lifted throughout friends, family and work

Happiness
Is being at peace with oneself
Being able to find who oneself really is
Understanding that the past has helped you grow

Being able to look to the future and work towards it

Thursday, 25th July 2013 - My Angel, My Rock & Me

Something to add to this, I have been saved so many times, to be honest whether you are religious or not there is someone with you to help you through it all

As the feathers of my angel are with me
Ever present within my life
They are soft, white and around me
With a never ending subtlety
Of always being there

For the next time I may fall
When they next pick me up
Whilst I next brush myself down
It will help to pick up strength
So that it can hold me tight

The feathers may not envelope me
Not all of the time
But when it is there I can feel it
The soft whispers of encouragement in my ear
Which echo throughout my life

It has seen me through bad times
Through good times
It will never leave me
I may hold it's wing after a trip
And be wrapped up when I fall

My angel holds me through the pain
Knowing that one day
One day I will not need her quite so much
At this time I call on her every day
I know that in my future she will be able to let go

I have seen someone come out
Out of unfurled wings around him
He is my rock and one I look towards
He encourages me
Makes and takes each baby step with me

He is an angel in human form
One who helps me take each step I make
Understands what is underneath
Sees the pain and helps me through
Helping me to make the picture for the future

I have other friends who are my angels in disguise
All of these help me through
The support I receive to take me through
Through to where I have to go
Where my life is going to lead me

Every time I take a step back
I know I will carry on forward
Because I know that it is a rest
There is nothing wrong with this
It helps me to contemplate what is next.

Reach out and talk
Talk to someone
With somebody
It doesn't matter how
Talking or writing it is such a good therapy

With this all in mind
I know I will get through
My angel
My rock

And Me

Friday, 26th July 2013 - Dare you...To Relax?

Close your eyes with me, I want to take you somewhere where I have been, somewhere you want to go, hold my hand let me guide you, relax: -
Dare you?

I dare, why not come out with me.
Take a walk on the wildlife side
Peek at the sunshine around the corner
Watch the animals
Take in the fresh air.

There is a bumble bee landing on the dog rose
And a beautiful Peacock butterfly on the buddleia
That is just the first few steps into the garden
Look at the roses and the honeysuckle
Take in the scent

Feel the sun's rays lifting a little of that cloud
Watch the goldfinch fly by you
And the robin pecking on the ground
Watch the glowing colours as you reach the garden gate
Just a short walk towards the open fields

Look at the yellow of the rapeseed
The greens of the grass and the trees
With the Red Kite flying above you
And the House Martin's fleeing their nests
Watch out or you will miss the Buzzard in front of you as well

Breathe in the fresh air and watch around you
Flies buzzing around with the bees and the wasps
The Bumble capturing every bit of pollen from the flowers
The Thunder daisies blowing in the breeze
As you see the wheat blowing around gently

See the white clouds floating by in the blue sky
Now listen for the singing
Singing of the different birds
The different sounds of the insects all around
Now I dare you just one smile

Keep walking around
Breathing in the fresh air around you
Take in the rays
Say hello to the passers by
Don't care what they say, you are doing all this for you
Relax as you see the butterfly dance

You hear a dog barking
Even see a squirrel scurry up the tree
All because they see a beautiful person smiling
Keep on walking
Turn around and we will walk back now

You have been out for a walk
It has been such a beautiful day
I know it doesn't help
You have had relaxation, exercise and chill time
We will take same route back seeing different things

As you look around
You will see a wasp
Don't be scared it won't hurt you
Look up in the tree you see a Kestrel
Quiet not to disturb, he frightens easily

There is a couple of Swallows flying above in the blue yonder
And the Sparrows with the Wood Pigeons singing away
As the afternoon comes closer to eve
You open your garden gate
Seeing the bees clambering around the Globe Thistles

As you walk up the path
You brush past the Clematis
As the colourful Laburnum grows over the archway
Take a very big breath
Think about what a wonderful walk you have been on

Next time take your camera
You have seen such wondrous things
They need recording tomorrow
Think how it has cleared your head

Now write about it anywhere
Look it up in the books
The dark cloud lifted slightly
You will hopefully feel peaceful by now
Don't fall asleep
You want to be able to do that tonight

Do one of your hobbies
Or talk to one of your friends
About what amazing things you have seen
How the walked helped lift you
I won't say it will cure, because it won't, it will help

Thank you for that walk

Saturday, 27th July 2013 - Life Will Get Brighter

Living with me has not been easy and I know it won't be for a while, but, I have a very patient and loving person by my side, with a few friends to help me, so I am very lucky as I know there are others who don't. All I can ask is try to find a support someone who has every faith you will come out of this or will stand by your side what ever comes to you: -

Take hold of your photos
The photos of the memories
Photos that cause your pain
Cut them up into pieces don't throw them away

Pick up the pieces and spread them around
Put them to places that make time
Time easier to control the pain inside
So you can move on to something happier

Take a look
What you have created
A Photo of your own
That can help your new future

Take the time to look inside
The pain has eased
The cloud is starting to lift
Now you can start to find your way

A way for you to look in the mirror
Turn the picture around
See what is behind
The mirror that has grown with the picture

Look into it
You will see the beautiful person on the outside
Take another look and smile
That is the person on the inside

You have grown such a strength
Such a beauty
That you can now stand tall

Take the next step into your new future
Every so often
You will look Back
Back to the past that used to be too painful
You will see the memories you placed in your own picture

Every so often
You will see the people
People who didn't understand or gave you the pain
You left them behind for a reason so you could move on

I know what I am doing
I am placing my picture together
So that one day
The pain will not be so painful

I can finally say thank you
Instead of regretting what has happened
Thank you for giving me my future
And letting go of what had happened to me

I still have the memories
I always will, so will you
They will grow easier instead of so painful
I will be able to look at what I had then and have now

The darkness of my pictures
Are getting lighter as I take them again
As I walk in nature with my new life
Whilst I learn about me being me

I have missed part of this
There are still some habits I cannot break
Slowly I will
And it will get easier, so will life to live with me

Saturday, 27th July 2013 - One Beautifully Strong Seed

I want to show you what you can do and be:-

There's a seed
Plant it in the garden
Water it
Watch it grow as the months pass by

As the summer comes
So do it's leaves
The branches strengthen
Then there are buds

With the sun
Each bud comes out
Flowers into a beautiful rose
Your favourite colour

Feel the petals
Look at the leaves
See the beauty
Mirroring in each flower

See the bees carrying the pollen
And the butterflies admiring the beauty
Look at that one strong rose
It is standing right in the centre

Just as you standing in the middle of the crowd
The others looking at you not understanding
As they old flowers all start to drop away
You are left with a few flowers around you to help and support you

The few flowers left will support you
Until you have the strength to go on on your own
They will stay with you as friends
You are and never will be alone

As the rain starts to fall
Keep watching the flowers around you
How strong you are to keep going
No matter what comes snow or shine

Someone will pick you as a flower
Because you have been so amazing and beautiful
There will be other flowers with you
Whatever path you take there is someone with you

Take care of that bush
Prune it back in the winter
Next spring will be the same
During that time you will rest and relax to start again on your next path

Your life will take many paths
As the years go by
Never worry about this

As this is where life will take you

Sunday, 28th July 2013 - Shout About It! (not a poem)

I don't think I need to say much more that my piece doesn't :-

I have sat listening to a lot of music lately and nothing has touched me more than two pieces Sound of Silence by Simon & Garfunkel and Read All About It Pt III by Emeli Sande.

Hello darkness, my old friend - the opening line to Sound of Silence, if you have not heard it before, then do it now from Youtube or look at the lyrics. I take the first line as my depression or the low moods with the darkest cloud, but it is sung in such a way that you would think it was nice to be there. Listen to and hear the lyrics it is sad with a certain hollowness, which is just how most of us feel.

We feel this because nobody is listening, understanding or hearing what we say. The darkness and the silence that all or a lot of us suffer, is so lonely, but, as I have said all or a lot which means none of us are alone, we stand behind a our own walls it isn't until we take out a brick or even make a hole in that wall we can see just a little light or be heard.

The silence of Mental Health is too silent we need to shout about it, we need to start talking openly as we do any other illnesses that have now been brought to the forefront of the media. We need to stand up and be counted with it, but, most of all let our MH illnesses be heard. We don't want or need sympathy, we want to be understood by others.

The more we talk about Mental Health Illness on any level the more we will be understood and the more done to help us keep in work, to be able to get help when we need it so there is flexibility and equality without the confusion or laughter of others because of medication, but, we expect to be treated fairly to make up time if needed.

Take out a brick from your wall and call out to someone only then will you find something that you need, the only way that you will hear, or can listen. The only thing is that it must start with us, nobody can do anything unless we ourselves do something first.

We have to begin by talking to someone, so they know and understand what is happening, who? You say, a friend, a family member and/or your GP. Believe it or not you will not know what they are going to say until you speak to them, the GP who I saw was brilliant, he sent me to counselling first, then when I went back after for a review he gave me medication, but, gave me numbers and organisations to help me more, things that can help me with CBT online things to get me through until counselling could start.

If you have a partner, girlfriend or boyfriend, wife or husband talk to them, help them to understand that you are not in a bad mood or just a low mood, tell them that there are other things attached to it, you can't sleep because of the things that are going through your head, not because you don't want to. That you are crying because you can't help it, that you are crying for some reason, but, don't know why. You aren't eating much or even eating more than you would usually. Or even don't want to go out and meet people.

The first thing I will say is you aren't alone and there at least 1 in 4 people who suffer from a mental health illness on some level and even more who are or have suffered in the past, if you talk to the person next to you, in front of you, behind you, and the other side of you.

I know this is going to sound harsh and I will say what I have said before you are the only one that can take that first step to change your life. You may think that someone is going to do it for you as I have done for a lot of years, I have only over the past few realised that it is me and only me that can do it, your family and/or friends can push you, but, you have to tell them how you are feeling.

So now you have done that, you have found your voice to say I have a mental health illness, you feel weak, wrong, so so very wrong, you have done that one step which is one massive step towards trying to help yourself and I commend you for this, it is a strength one strength that will grow as you work through.

There are so many different Mental Health Charities who need help, not just in volunteering time or helping to raise money, but for you to tell them your story, straighten yourself up pull your jacket down and get your email ready to write to them, write your story, we need to make a bigger hole in the wall, the wall that is in front of yours, the bigger picture of it all is...

WE NEED TO TALK AND SHOUT ABOUT MENTAL HEALTH ILLNESS

You've got the words to change a nation - The first line to my second song by Emeli Sande, Sit and listen to the song Read All About It PT III if you haven't before or even look up on the internet for the lyrics watch the video on Youtube.

Mental Health illness starts with you as I have said before, but, there are a lot voices wanting to break down the wall in front of theirs and slowly it is getting there.

Wanting others to understand is the first thing, that we aren't crazy, we aren't mad, just have a mental health illness. You want to carry on working through all of this, you can if you have an understanding manager, someone who you can discuss things with or a colleague who understands what is happening, it does help. Most of all it helps if your company has someone you can talk to just for a few minutes when you are having a low mood and need to talk to get it all out.

You want your friends and family to understand or hear what you are saying. For some of us this isn't easy especially if they don't see what happened, they don't want to hear what you have to say, they are telling you exactly what you don't want to hear "Snap out of it" or "Pull your socks up" or even "Leave the past behind you don't keep thinking about it" you think that I haven't had any of this, I have, but, this isn't stopping me from shouting about lifting Mental Health. I won't let it get me down, I have taken the step forward to get myself better.

You won't do it on your own, because as before there is someone out there who wants to hear and help you, someone who will understand. We don't want extra kindness or sympathy just understanding.

We want to inform others that Mental Health Illnesses won't just disappear, they are not to be laughed at especially if someone is sat crying at their desk or in their car, or sat with the duvet around them on their settee or bed, we want to talk about it openly, so that it can be understood
how, what , why and when so that we know what to do for someone else if we see it or to help ourselves in the future before we get down that road again.

My boyfriend had a Mental Breakdown, I have depression. I started this blog so that my voice can be heard, so I can talk about my feelings to help me get through depression and to help me support my life partner, telling of his experience through a supporter's point of view and now my own.

I want to say so much to all of you, the strength and the steps back, they will happen, tell someone express it whichever way you need to but talk to someone. I write poetry, take photos, writing my third book, make jewellery. I find that doing creativity helps my mind, because it is running at ten to the dozen, if it didn't come out with my fingers it would come out with my mouth and I don't say the right things or get out what I really mean.

The reason I do it in writing as well is so that I can tell others they are not alone, that there are others hearing and listening, willing to understand what they are saying no matter how manic or low you are, let the tears fall, scream as much as you want, we will get it heard one day and the wall will tumble down outside of our own walls until then we have to keep talking.

Be brave and talk to everyone, be your own hero which is what I think you are, you have taken that first step, now keep going, your strength will grow inside and out. You are a beautiful and amazing person whoever you are, we are all different in each way, but beautiful, amazing and strong, cry because that is a strength to be able to cry about it.

We all get through our days in whatever way, but, we need to say something loud and clear we are not crazy.

Help lift the stigma I say and *I wanna sing, I wanna shout, I wanna scream 'til the words dry out, So put it in all of the papers, I'm not afraid, They can read all about it, Read all about it,* from one of the verses by Emeli Sande, song may not have been written for this reason or Mental Health, but once you have read it, you will see what I mean.

We have to and need to lift the stigma, but, it starts with us!

A happy day, one of the few, but there will be more

Tuesday, 30th July 2013 - Disillusionments Or Freedom?

Well, here is just a little ditty that has come into my head full of hope and strength, that might help me and others to carry on.

At a time of disillusion
Of the illusions of the past
I feel the pieces pull together
As though, they never have

Whilst I sit and think about them
I feel the pain I had
But to them they want to beat me
Even though they are my past

I will not let them beat me
I will get through this fight
The one only way is to describe what I have had
Then the pieces will form my path

The path in my mind
Is to free myself from pain
With this is hope I to gain
My past life which will gradually wane

With the work I accomplish
The freedom from my past
So that I walk along
My Long and future path

With all this in mind
I have hope and faith
With the ability
To be able to find the strength as well

When all is said and done
My disillusionments of the past
Will not be bad

Because thanks to them I will have a long and happy life

Tuesday, 30th July 2013 - Stronger Glass

I don't know where it is all coming from please read on :-

Pull the blinds from my eyes
Let the sunlight in
Help me forget
Where I have been

Leave the past behind me
So that I can start again
It doesn't matter how much
Let the pain subside

Where there used to be darkness
Let there be light
So I can make sense
Of the thoughts that went in

I have bobbed from here
Bobbed to there
Now I know where I belong
But, now I have a steady place to stay

Where do I want to be
Anywhere in the light
What do I want to do
Anything except for pain

I have torn the bars from my hearts
Put wings on my back
Now I need to know
How not to go back

It is easy to say
Keep looking ahead
For some of us though
That is in our head

The only way to see is it
A each shard of glass breaks

I will pick it up carefully
Putting it in my stained glass picture
Hold on there
Please do not clear up my mess
This is for me to do
I do confess

I am the only one who knows
Where each piece of the glass goes
Walk on by or stand by my side
Support me until everything dies

One day
It will come together
The pieces glued
So I can look in the mirror

I will look at both sides of what I have made
Into the picture for the past
Into the mirror for how the future looks
Both sides are fragile but, with time will grow in strength

Thursday, 1st August 2013 - Fresh Start

I have been pretty poorly again over the past couple of weeks, I have also found something that could have helped my low moods, now I am on the right medication I am trying to take this new step:-

As I sit about the world wandering outside
Getting on with their own lives
Wishing that I could do the same
Stuck in my head

Let me out
Unlock the padlock
Throw away the key
Let the gate open

Pull the bars down
And leave a hole in my wall
One big enough for me to step through
Or even for the light to stream through

Let my darkness lift
Bit by bit
I know it will take time
To get to where I want

Step by baby step
I will follow my path
The long and winding path
To life's new bright future

One I have been waiting for
All my life
Where I can belong
Without looking back

If I do look back
I will only see the window
Stained glass window
Of the past that saved me for this

When I get there
I will thank you all
But in the meantime
I am just grateful for now

So many times
My angels have come to me
Come to save my sweet life
Now I am getting stronger for it

This is no weakness
It is a strength
One which I will not forget

In my new time

Thursday, 1st August 2013 - My Sunrise

This is how I perceive my first steps when I start take the walk through my steps with me:-

With peace and serenity
I am starting to see my life
With a different light
And a new path

With peace and serenity
I will breakdown the bars
Which have enclosed me
I will take them down one by one

As the bars come down
My tears will start to dry
And the curtains to be pulled back
With the sunshine peeking through

With the sunshine
There will be hope
A dawn to start the day
Ney, to start my life anew

Upon the sunrising
There will be a new path
Waiting to take me
To wherever I will go

The time will come
For the sun to set
But, that will be on the pain
The pain I have had from the past

No more the times
Will I look back to feel guilty
Or look back to hurt myself
I will look back to say that I am here

Here is a new place
I am looking around me
Take the first step

On the long journey ahead

Friday, 2nd August 2013 - A Letter of Understanding

(Not a poem)

I am not having to say much here just why? :-

Dear Friends, Colleagues and Family

I have depression. This is a mental illness that I am trying to control, at the moment I have it because I have had so much going on in my life that my head and body have said stop!! You need to rest, you need to take a moment to step back, look back, think about the past, put it into some place where you can handle it instead of thinking that you can just trundle through life wallowing in self pity.

This mental illness is not a weakness it is a strength to be able to say that you have to stop, you are burnt out from past happenings, past events, you cannot carry on going at full speed as you have done or are doing, time to kick off your shoes and think about where this past pain has taken you.

It is a very dark and for some a dangerous place, as long as we have the right people around us to get us through, we can place the pieces of the puzzle in the right places and stop self-indulging in our pain, for a lot of us it can take a few weeks, months, others, years or a lifetime of in and out, as long as we know how to handle the lifetime to be able to carry on we are alright.

The pains each of us have suffered are marriage rape, rape, sexual abuse, violent abuse, mind abuse, control freaks or anything else including the trappings of war or family problems including marriage break ups or problems at work ie bullying, stress etc.

None of this is easy to deal with if we didn't know who to turn to when it first happened to us or if there was nobody there for us. A lot of us have walked through our lives becoming lower and lower because there was nobody who understood, family, friend or even partners.

I have tried to kill myself twice and as I have said before I was saved each time by a friend and the fire service(I commend you and thank you). I have spoken to Samaritans in the past and I now have the best support I can get my partner, my best friend and a few new friends.

What I am so pleased to see is that there are still a lot of friends, mine and my partners who can snub us or avoid us because they think we are not normal, that they think they don't know what to say, what I would like to ask is have you tried? Have you even picked up the phone and asked us if we are alright? Have you asked us to come and have a beer? NO! you have not, so before you judge what we are like try talking to us instead of ignoring us, sit up and smell the roses, try to understand that what you are doing is making things worse. It may be one of you one day that could be in the same situation, see how you would feel if you didn't have your friends to help you nor family.

I have no family close by all I have are in Spain or US, I am relying on friends to help me instead of pushing me away, to understand what it is like to be going back over my life and picking up the glass that hurts me each time I look at it and being able to put it somewhere I can handle it in the future. You may not know what I have been through, but, again have you asked me?

It is all very well saying don't dwell on the past, carry on with the future, but, until my past is put away I can only move on slowly with my future. I want to stop crying for no reason, I want someone to tell me what triggers it all off, I know this only starts with me.

If I have to make changes, surely you as my friends and family can help and by doing that you have to first of all ask me what depression is and understand it. I want you to ask me what has happened to be so painful in my past that all of a sudden I have come to this letter to you.

Nobody is listening, I want you all to listen, hear and understand what we are all saying to each other, do you think we want to wallow in self-pity or self-obsess about our past, no, we would like to get past it all and lead our lives normally, if you heard or listened to what we were saying to help us in the right direction, going to a group with a friend, having a coffee or a beer with a friend and listening to even the hardest of their memories, you never know what could happen

Make a difference today, if it is a long time since you have spoken to someone who says they have depression ask them to sit and talk to you about it, understand what they are saying, ask questions, if they can't answer then there will be someone who will.

This goes for anyone who is low at all, you don't know what their circumstances or problems are, do it before they tell you they are ill.

Look it up from the internet, it doesn't matter, we all need to talk to people, this is just the craziest of illnesses that if you don't pick it up early enough you get dragged down. Don't let it do it to you or your friends, but help someone else, talk to your friend help them so that you can both understand and help each other.

My life has been turned upside down by this several times and I hate it. I have found this a good therapy to talk to people. I am hoping that today I am going to reach to the right people, the ones that need to help those who have Mental Illness if not, put the piece in front of them to help them understand so that you can talk to them, cry on their shoulders whatever, make them understand what you are going through.

My Name is Susan Bell, I am 42 years old, I am a writer, an author and blogger to reach out for mental health, I suffer from depression because of marriage rape, family problems, control freaks, emotional and mental abuse and the last marital breakdowns.

Now I am with a wonderful understanding man, who is guiding me through as I have guided him through his break down. And I am on my first step to recovery, each baby step I will get there.

Thank you for hearing what I have to say.

Heartily Mindful

Friday, 2nd August 2013 –

My Time has Come To Start Walking My Path!

How I perceive how or where I have got to with my first steps - not far, but, it is only baby steps and I will finally get there:-

Crash!!
Did you hear that?
Because I felt it
Crash!! what the heck is going on

For every step I am going through
Inside my head
There is a crash
When I take each step I turn around and pick up the pieces

The fragments of time
Shards of glass from the pictures
Pictures I once held in my memory
Ones that used to be held close to my heart

As I pick up the pieces
I can throw some away
Some of them like faces will have to be placed
In the bigger picture

Once that bigger picture is formed
It will be easier to look at
Memories easier to talk about
When you walk beside me to ask you will find out

My hand is held
So that I don't go back to the place
The places and times that hurt too much
It is there to steady me and help me if I cry

The music I hear
One or two pieces I love
Take me back
Trying to put it into place so I can hear it again

One day
I will be able to see it and hear the old music
I will be able to dance to it
Will be able to show it and talk about it

What I hear now is new
New music with a new dance
Which I am being taught new steps to
Slowly, sometimes I still stop and start again

When all the picture is finished
There will be a beautiful and strong woman behind it
Facing me in the mirror
At the moment I can't look

If you want to walk with me
Or even come and talk with
I am happy for you to
I would like to help you understand

Understand the world that I am and have been in
Yes, it has been mine
But, until I was rested I could never move on
I had to think about how I was going to move on

Now I have taken the time to think about it
Time to sit down write, relax and think
It is time now for me to get out from all of this darkness
Move into the light again

Make the tears stop rolling
The hurt stop the pain
The past to start my future over again
I will leave who I need to leave behind

My Time has Come To Start Walking My Path!

Wednesday, 7th August 2013 - My First Step

Well, I took my first step and a big one it was:-
My head has been a mess
Since the day I did confess
That I could no longer do my job
Which was causing me so much stress

I walked into work
Explained why I had been ill
Then admitted that I could no longer
Go on

Try doing it
It hurts
You think it would be easy
It wasn't

What I have done is struggled
Struggled with what is happening next
What I want to do
Where I want to go

I know that I was lost
Not even keeping my head above water
I could only just paddle
I couldn't get through it

The thoughts that were racing
The memories no erasing
Trying to help myself come to terms
With what my head wants to do

That was the first step
So now I have to take the next
To get myself to be me again
To stop being so serious

The little black cloud hovering around me
Will one day leave me
So that I can be the bright
Ray of sunshine as I was

Wednesday, 7th August 2013 - My Clearing Path

The fog that was once so thick is slowly starting to clear even though I still don't know
where I am going yet, but, with some guidance and application I will:-

My Eyes have opened up
Even if it is ever so slightly
To see the light outside
Outside my inside
To see what is happening

I have caused mayhem
For all those around me
But, have helped to soothe myself
To finally give myself a little peace

Peace inside
Calm in my rest
I still feel the rough
And I will take it with the smooth
The smooth of the peace

The first step I took
It was a new path
A path that was hard to take
But, if I needed fresh
Someone will guide me

I have my angels
Calming my peace
Enveloping me in their wings
The sunshine will start
When I finally know

I still know though
The inner peace that I will get
When I am finally finished
Will help me through
Will put the pieces in my picture

The picture I will be able to look back on
The thoughts that raced through my head
The day before

Have calmed, there are still some there
But the peace I feel is better

There will be a day when I know
Know why I myself
Have been saved
And what stopped me from doing anything

My Path will clear with the fog around my thoughts one day

Thursday, 8th August 2013 - My New Waltz

I want to show you that you can have peace and tranquility in your life if you allow it, go for a walk and think about it, let the light shine down as your new music begins and the notes of the past become all jumbled so you no longer hear them any longer:-

As I Sit here writing
I feel a tranquillity in my heart
One of peace
That will form my path

The path I shall walk
Slowly into my new light
Along with the people
Who want to stand by my side

As I make each step
And slow each thought
To try and walk
My way with my talk

I also stop
To think about my short hop
A hop across the life
Which I am making for me

See how it shapes
Watch the picture I make
Let the pieces fall into place
At each step I take

I am thinking about me
Wanting my life to be better
Not to be too far apart
From the tale I am about to start

I have pain in my heart
Which I am trying to help
With each new note I hear
I make the new dance to start

There are only few people
Who understand
But, I no longer what to remain here
Underneath this dark cloud

Let the light come in
And the music begin
Whilst the waltz is learnt
Let my old picture form

Friday, 9th August 2013 - Time To Talk (Not a poem)

Well, I don't think there is an explanation needed for my post today except come by add a comment and talk to me on my Heartily Mindful Facebook Page or a tweet on twitter for Heartily Mindful, because my friends it is #Time to talk about what so many of us hide inside:-

Dear Me

How did you get where you are now?

What became of you?

What chemical imbalance made you snap to such a low place?

The answers are all in my head somewhere, but, what I can tell you is I am not enjoying sitting here and writing under such a black cloud.

The cloud I would love to blow over me like the wind is blowing the trees outside. I do know is that I have a lot of people holding me close, holding my hand as I step each stone of my new pathway to help and support me.

There are some people I have had to leave behind, some I believed to be friends and ones that would stand by me, but, they haven't in fact they have just gone by the way side my mind has had to push them out to a picture which I can look at again.

The shards of glass from my future have been left lying around on the ground, they have cut my feet, they have hurt my heart, now though I have to look towards the light shining outside of this cloud and start to put my past memories somewhere I can look at them to thank them for where they have got me.

It isn't great having all this pain inside you have to find somewhere to put it, you have to look back and think if there is something that can be done to help yourself get out of the dark cloud hanging over you, to stop you triggering into a low mood, something that might help you place that memory in a better place so it won't hurt so much next time you look at it or you see something that will be a trigger.

My belief is that there is a place in which you can do this to help you recover and it has taken me a very long time to realise it, there will be still the times it may hit a bone inside especially if someone starts saying something or opposing what that that pain is inside, you will feel like getting angry and screaming. The only thing I can say is take a deep breath, either put up a good argument or say to yourself not to listen and they haven't been where you have.

I am not a counsellor, I am not a medicine person, but, I have experience through my own depression. I am having to learn the hard way. Making mistakes, picking up the threads and putting everything back together in the right place, somewhere I can face things.

I have started to become a stronger person by realising that I have to face everything head on, the only way I can stop the pain is by tearing that memory into pieces and putting them into my picture or even smashing the glass and picking up a piece at a time, putting it next to something nice that will help me to get around it, something that will stop me from see the whole horrible sordid tale again without the pain inside. I am starting to get the picture, looking at the bigger picture, not just looking at mine, looking at the one with my partner, as he helps me to piece it together I will realise how these memories have got me to him.

I have been mislead, misguided, tagged along, or even pulled in a lot of directions in my lifetime by a lot of different people which is what has caused me to live my life the way I have. Now I have the chance to do this my way not hide away as I have before, I suppose you could say that for two of them I had before I have tried killing myself, but, I would never do it again, no matter how much I thought about it, why you ask? Because I have found the one person that allows me to be me and expects nothing from me or me from him.

We have been together for a year now, neither one of us have left each other's sides. We have gone through each other's mental illnesses. He has now come out the other side and he is encouraging me out from my density of wood with whatever he can for me, allowing me to come out of myself on my own.

I may only have been through something small compared to others who are reading this, but, I encourage you and implore you to start pushing the bricks from the walls that surround you, to shout out and try as hard as possible to not care what anyone else says, you may be able to find a person who finally hears what you say, the one person that will make you stand up and think what you have done for yourself by saying something.

It is time to talk, it doesn't matter who, just talk let it all out, let ourselves be heard.

What we have is an illness like any other illness it is triggered by several chemical reactions, we don't have diabetes, but, we want to be heard as diabetics are heard. There is no explanation as to why, but, it just happens, we don't want sympathy, just want to be heard by people to be understood and live our lives the same as others do.

It is time to talk.

Talk to someone who understands. Help someone else to understand.

Time to talk

About what is happening to us and how if things changed or we were understood we wouldn't be shouting so much. We need help not to be thought that we are crazy.

It is time to talk

We are humans as well, humans with problems not to be blanked because you can't or don't understand
#Time to talk

Please talk to me about whatever your story is it doesn't matter how small or big, I want to hear, I want to help.

I want to save at least one person from being ignored. Remember I understand, so talk to me

My name is Susan Bell, I am a depression sufferer, I have helped my partner through his own mental breakdown.

Talk to me.....Because it is time to talk(anonymously if you want to)

Friday, 9th August 2013 - Hear The Peace Around You

Don't let time take over the pain that has just been caused, if you leave it the more it will hurt, try talking about it before the pain hurts too much:-

Silence from the clock
As it stands in the corner
Nothing can be heard
Not even a Tick Tock

Time stood still
Take a look around
See what you can see
Feel what you can feel

Watch the clouds
Out of the window
Still floating, but not going by
There is no wind

Now see the people
They have all stood still too
Nobody moving
The cars are in a dream

What you see
With your eyes all around
Is time stood still
No moving on

Scarier and scarier
How could it happen
This is how your mind sees the world
Stood still in history

Can you feel the pain
The pain of yesterday
When that memory happened
You wished for time to stand still

So that you didn't have to keep thinking
Think about what had happened
Instead you need to shatter the memory now
Pick up the pieces and place them again

Place them so that you can deal with that pain now
You have to look at the pain now
So that it doesn't hurt you anymore
Or rule any part of your life

Your life will change
Except it is now you have dealt with it
So you can move on with ease
So you can start the new dance again

Listen to the music
It has changed
The steps are different
Because you took the pain straight away

Listen to the beat
It's in rhythm with the time
The time of the ticking clock
Everything is now able to move again

That was easier
Than dealing with it too late
When it would hurt too much
The pain is still there just easier to deal with

Listen to the music
To dance with the rhythm of the beat
Take the hands of the person
Who can help you to take the new steps

Hear the peace around you

Friday, 9th August 2013 - Dream of the Day

One of my old time things of it getting to this time of night to those who know or
remember –

I have just watched
The most wondrous colours in the sky
Colours that showed how beautiful tomorrow
To sit out in the garden
Watching the bees going by

I don't watch people
I watch nature
You sit and wish how you could be like them
With not a care in the world
Where you could fly away

Where the colour flowers
Would beckon you
To the reds, blues and pinks
What a wondrous world it would be
To fly around and see so much

So much more than we do
Going to the smaller holes
Having fun with friends
Working so hard
And talking so much

Being able to see what is around
Next time sit in the garden and close your eyes
Listen to the noises
The whispers and the chatter from nature
From all around you

Smell the beautiful scents that are in and around
Feel the wind blow
As it does smell again the more scents blown across
Sit into the evening and watch
Watch the blanket over this side of the world

So that we can sleep
With all the fresh air inside our lungs
The delicious fragrances from the day
And the feel of the grass below our feet
We will be able to sleep now peacefully underneath the blanket

Dream of the day

Saturday, 10th August 2013 - Make a difference it is #TimeToTalk

Click on the links in my post and you will get to any of the websites that will help you

Dear Life and heart

Please could you give me this one last chance to change, change for the better, I am so tired of living in the same day, day in day out under this black cloud and within the four walls that have built up over time.

I want to stop the silence that rings in my ears with such deftness, such a loud sound that I cannot hear anything not even my own voice, not even the voices of the friends and family around me who want to help me. I know that until I admit I need help and I ask for it I will not get it

I have sometimes been at the edge that I no longer want to go on, that I want to hurt you my life and stop you, my heart from beating the blood around my body. I want to stop these feelings, I don't know what to do or how to do this, I have to break this cycle of disliking myself and start looking for help from outside of my own four walls where I have been stuck for too long.

If I change first of all by giving myself the chance, perhaps taking a step outside the door, if I take a look around and nobody is there I can walk, if I was to take some music with me, perhaps that might help, yes, let's make the first step the first step outside of my comfort zone, a step where I can actually bare what I have been under, yes I am thinking about myself, to get back into the big wide World in my own way.

If I hold my hand out and start talking is this a step in the right direction, I am always being told to talk, but, who to, who wants to hear what I have to say is there anyone who understands, anyone who wants to understand or hear what I have to say

I don't know what to say to people do I tell them everything or just how I am feeling? I don't know where to start?

I want to be heard by people and with the talking I want to change the way my life is at the moment, to be able to step outside and feel the sunshine. I want to be able to talk to my friends again and go out have a laugh, not sit under my duvet or watching television.

Let's just start by putting some music on, I will pick up my phone, look at my computer and see who has been trying to call me, I will try to call them back and have a coffee with them or even talk to someone online, perhaps that would be a start. So many thoughts running through my head, I don't know where to start and then I never start.

I will start with trying to talk to someone from Elefriends and see what they suggest. Talk to my doctor and then talk to my nearest friend. As I start to slow you down heart and the thoughts slow, so does my breathing.

Turn on the music, turn on my laptop and talk to an elefriend, look at my long list of emails, and facebook messages.
Turn on my phone and talk to someone, make an appointment with my doctor. It is time to make the change and #TimeToTalk to someone. Time to make a difference in my life and perhaps in someone elses, all I have to do is click #TimeToTalk and it will take me to somewhere that will help.

I feel it is time to change not only my life, others as well by telling them what is happening to me, let my life and heart start to live again, no matter how low, when I get to be able to ask for help or for someone to understand me the low times won't seem so bad, because I will have someone to talk about them.

Take a look at me, what has happened in my past I want to shatter into a thousand pieces and put it all back together again. I am still the same person, but unless I change even one thing in my life it will still keep happening to me.

I have made so many bad decisions, based on what others have told me or have controlled me that now I have the chance to change all that, one step on my own and the next with a friend beside me.

One day I will change to the beautiful person in the mirror behind the mosaic from my past, I will see what is changing like a butterfly coming from the chrysalis to fly freely into my future. I can see a light and another path for myself I just have to start to walk it. I know I will need help.

I want to help others as I am doing this, I don't want them to feel they are in such a situation they can't get out of it. I want to help others manage their mental health so that they can live their lives to the fullness that they can.

I don't want to see people struggling I want them to see it is #TimeToTalk go to a friend, doctor, Mind, Rethink, Blurt It Out, Elefriends and lots more just click on the links and I will soon get some help so will you.

Live your life and you will soon start to love it again, start the change and you will be in a position to love it again, you will find someone, friends, family, health practitioner or even an online friend.

This has been my first step to change my life and heart with every hope that my mind will start to peaceful so that I can make the other changes that are needed in my life.

Thank you me for wanting to make these changes and that I have another chance to make these changes.

My name is Susan Bell, I am 42 years old and I am a depression sufferer who has supported her 43 year old partner through his mental breakdown and I have made the first step to making the change in my life giving me another chance to help you with your life.

Make a difference it is #TimeToTalk

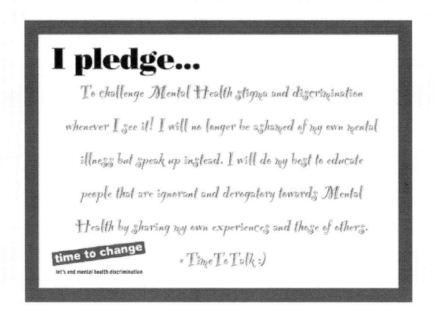

Saturday, 10th August 2013 - From An Old Path To The New

I have made so many different changes today no matter how small, they are big enough to start with:-

Wow
Today started my journey of change
There are so many changes we need to make
To get us to where we need to be
Where we want to be

Take a look around you
At the flowers that open daily
The bees that fly around
Birds that are always chasing food
We are always watching in awe and wonder

The trees that open and shed their leaves
That grow the fruit as it falls
Where the children bend down to pick it up
What we eat in our time
When do we know what change to make

We have to be the masters of our changes
The people who change and know what we change
Look around and see how we can change things
Watch the children whose past lies ahead of them
And the future that is about to pass them to make memories

Our pathways our mapped out for us
But it is up to us to change
Change what we need to change to make a difference
To shout if we need to
Or even talk where we want to and have to

We need to wake up to our own reality
To what we need to do to help people with their change
As well as our own change
There are things in our past that will hurt
Until we face them, we cannot place them

Place our hurt and fears somewhere
Somewhere we can see them
Where they will no longer hurt so much
The pain will not go away
It will ease and each time we will say it has got me where I am today

You and I are strong enough
Strong enough to get past these fears and pain
The old memories that once made us weak have now given us strength
Strength to walk on
Walk on along this path, the new path our old life has put us on

The old path has now joined your bright new path to our future

Sunday, 11th August 2013 –

Time To Change No Matter How Small (Not a Poem)

I would like to tell you where change and how changes can make a difference or make a difference for mental health, please do not hesitate to comment
Changes - what a word, it can be meant for so many things in this time.

Definition of Change - to become different; to become altered or modified; to become transformed or converted; to pass gradually into; to make a change or an exchange.

Think about the definitions before you read my piece what Changes means for you?

What could it mean for you?

Is there anything you can do to change even one thing to be different to now?

For me it can be the changes I have made in a lot in fact feels like too many in my lifetime. I think there are a lot of us who have had or had to make a lot of changes in our lives.

Change of mental health, job, lifestyle, partners, independence for marriage or marriage for independence, friends, school, habits, food, medicines, countries, having children, losing children, losing control, gaining control, being in love, hating someone you really should love, finding a true love, parents, losing parents, having pets, losing pets, controlled relationship, being able to do what you want without a question, I think that I could fill another page or two, but, I'm not going to you get the idea of what I am saying.

Some of these memories are locked away in the back of our heads some of them will stay there, but, others will be triggered one day by something or our chemistry imbalances for some reason and they all come flooding out, which is why we find it hard to lock it all away again.

Changes for me in my lifetime have been a lot and I have had a hard time to deal with them, but, I am trying to find a way of doing it so that I can face my new life with my new man(year old relationship) with as little as possible so that I can tell him everything without the tears flooding and the anger hyped up inside of me about the memories.

I may not be able to change these painful memories, if I can't I will pull them apart and put them in a place where I can bare to talk about them openly, I was going to do today, but, it was too painful, I will do it one day.

The memories for me are losing friends from moving around, marriage rape, controlling relationships, changing schools and leaving friends behind, losing friends, men making decisions for me that were wrong, not allowing myself to be able to move on in my life and standing still moving on to the next one. Having depression and having people who do not understand around me within friends or men. Changing in my body due to illnesses.

You see I have had a lot of changes to deal with, some I cannot change and others I can. Those I cannot change I am starting to accept I can't, however as you see above I am learning to manage it as I have to because otherwise I will do the same as what one of those changes is saying that I will never move on from my past, this time though is so much different, because I have someone who understands my illness to be able to help me move on.

Someone who loves me for being me with or without depression and is willing to hold my hand all the way, help me to manage it if it is a long term imbalance. I helped him through his breakdown and then I started to sit in a corner, crying and angry at myself, not knowing what to do because I didn't want to feel inside except numb to hide the pain and my feelings. He woke up one day to see what he had seen in himself and told me he was strong enough to help me make my changes.

He said that the changes he had made to help himself were nearly done and he was ready to help me start to make my changes, the changes I needed to be me again, to see me smiling all the time again, to hear me laughing, but I do already do this, except I am me with a low mood.

I was happy to admit it, but, I was hoping that he was strong enough to support me, because I could no longer support him the way I was before, he said me being there was all the support he needed now and I still talked to him, it was enough as he was strong enough.

You see what I am trying to say is that one step in change is talking to someone, admitting your mental illness so they can help you to the next step, this is the strongest step you will take because you are finally admitting you need help and there is something wrong, there is no weakness in admitting any of it, it is a strength and a change.

There are so many that hide behind not wanting to make this change, because they are afraid of what everyone is going to say to them, your friends and family would have seen it and don't be afraid you aren't alone in wanting to make this one change. The change might hurt, but, it is for the good.

There are so many changes in life even in the World.
The World of Mental Health is always changing and so are the medications, but, the ones we want to make are to say that we who have a mental health illness do not get misunderstood, that we can make the changes by helping others, by telling our own stories with or without the changes we have made, with preferably so that we can show how we can move on by either management of our illness or changing our lives.

We need to be able to lift this crazy thing they think that we deserve to only be locked up, that it is all in our heads and we shouldn't live normal lives. We have to help with the change in the World's thinking of Mental Health illnesses on whatever level, that we are not mad and we cannot just click our fingers and get better on their say so.

We want those who don't understand what lies beneath is not just what happened in our lives it is a chemical imbalance that has thrown us off course and we want to find our way back, we can't always do it and we have to learn to manage it, some of us can and some of us can't, we no longer wanted to be segregated as barmy, nuts, it is just in our heads. We don't want to cry and shout, we don't want to have a really good week and then go back to an all time low. We just want to be treated as someone with diabetes does to be understood for our chemical imbalance or genetic frailties.

Take a look at me and see what you see from the photo below do you see any difference do I look abnormal :-

I know, I look mad, insane, as though I should just snap out of it. How would you know if I wasn't in the middle of an episode of mania or just normal or even being allowed to laugh at something whilst I was with my partner.

Think about how you could change this, how you would want your workplace to change, do they need more understanding or training to work with mentally ill colleagues without judgement, no bullying, no laughing at how we all act. I have just left a workplace like that behind me who do not understand what was going on, because I didn't think I can tell them. I made the decision to leave it and make this my stand that I will help anyone with mental health illness be heard.

I would say even some agencies have a little to learn about avoiding candidates with mental health illnesses, thinking they are incapable of working in fact we probably work better and a lot harder because we want to prove we can manage our illnesses, all I ask is for a chance.

Well, most of you know who I am just to say my name is Susan Bell, I am 42 years old I have depression, I have supported my 43 year old partner through his mental health illness.

We both stand to help raise stigma from mental health illnesses, giving mental health illness an awareness and to help others make changes in their our lives no matter how small or large.

It is Time to Change with #TimeToTalk

Thank you for reading

Sunday, 11th August 2013 - A Haunting Prospect

My walk this afternoon -

I have just walked
Around a peaceful bit of wilderness
One which none of us really wants to go
The silence is so deafening
You will only ever hear the haunting of the church bells

As the grey stones lay
All lined up in a row
The sunshine down on the place
The place where we wanted to go
To lay some flowers on a grave

Yes, it was a graveyard
Where we have just been
To pay our respects on his fathers birthday
He would have been the ripe old age of 81 today
Do you know what we talked, smiled and lay the flowers down

As we walked around the church grave yard
My partner found others that he knew
Knew had killed themselves at such an early age
Reminding us how lucky we are
To have someone to talk to when they didn't

The reason why I am saying this
Is because I feel sad about it
As we walked around we sat on his father's bench
Which had been sent from the hospital when it changed used
This was from people whom loved him very much

People who are always around us
To let us know we are not alone
Never think you are
Because there is always someone
Someone you can talk to even the Samaritans or an Elefriends online

I want you know what my partner's dad didn't know
He probably didn't realise and none of us do until it's too late
How many love you
My Partner's dad died from cancer
But just remember the lady I mentioned earlier who left her children behind

There is no need to feel alone
There is always someone to talk to
No matter how near or far
I only want to enter that graveyard for one person
Not have to remember too many.

The time has come to end
This solemn little ditty
What I really want you to remember
Is it is #TimeToTalk

There are so many organisations to talk to

Monday, 12th August 2013 - Starry Night, Oh in Awe

I can now hear the toot of the tawny owl outside of my window as I write this short post
to you tonight, my head has been so full of stupid things today and it has been going
from one to another thing :-

What a starry night
Go and gaze upon them
You never know what you may see
I have seen so much already

Take a gaze at the World up above
They look like a glitter ball
All around us
Twinkling away in the bright moonlight

Look and watch at midnight
You will see a meteor shower falling
I have already been out to watch
I have seen four falling with a friend stood with me

The wonderment of the colour of the sky
The clouds that were covering
And the planets hovering around us
Let it relax your mind

Think about the colours you are watching
What is flowing
Take a deep breath and be in awe

Of what you may find

Tuesday, 13th August 2013 - Until Calmness is Bestowed

This is exactly how my head starts to move, until someone tells me to calm down and relax take a deep breath and start again:-

Where to stop
Where to begin
Oh my goodness
My head is in such a spin

Thoughts darting around
Calm down up there
Let me slow down
So I can just think here

When the words start to pour
From my very core
That is where all my words
Will hold in a fore

When do you stop
As the clock tick tocks
Or do you start
With the beat of your heart

When I hear the minutes
They pass like seconds
And the hours pass like minutes
When will it ever finish

Slow my heart
Hear my thoughts
I want them to be put in order
So I can carry on without disorder

I flitter here
Flitter there
Settle down
As I try to think up there

My mind starts to slow

And so does my body
As I try to assemble
How I want to think

The calmness of the music
A touch of a hand
Starts to put my mind to rest
As it slows I hear order

Thank you for the hand that has touched me
For the music around me
The order of my thoughts
I can stop and begin to think again

Madness I call it madness
It is just the way my thoughts tend to go
Hither and thither

Until calmness is bestowed

Tuesday, 13th August 2013 – Silence With The Peace Of The Night

Watch the sky tonight you should see more of the star studded heavens and the meteor shower:-
Silence around me
In my head
My heart and deep down
Inside my soul

This peace has come
After a day of racing thoughts
What to do
Where to go

When they calm
As they have in now
I am in awe of the silence
Surrounding me

I can hear the night time noises
Not just the voice in my head
It gives me time to slow
Slow down to the relaxation I need

Perhaps it will be a peaceful night
Try it
Stop and close your eyes
Hear what is around you

If there is too much noise turn it off
Listen to what is outside
Look out to the stars if you can
Show them you are in awe

What a beautiful black velvet
Studded with diamonds
With one big pearl sat in the centre
Watch the meteor rocket by

Look out again tonight and enjoy the night

Wednesday, 14th August 2013 –

Stepped Outside The Comfort Zone

I have stepped outside my comfort zone today, broadened my horizons :-

The hustle and bustle
Started today
With telephone calls everywhere
Not knowing if I was coming or going

My head hurts so much
It is in a whirl
I know that with this
Swirling around is a new beginning

I am starting along my new pathway
Where my history has had a part to play
So whatever has happened to me
Has helped me get where I am

It has shaped my life enormously
To how people see me
The perspective of employers
Is a good perspective

Even though my CV does not look healthy
I have been told not to sell myself short
Which is what I have been doing
Your past path has shaped you to what you are today

Put some confidence in yourself
Stand tall
You are better than you think you are
Hold your head up high

Shout about yourself
Don't get pulled in by what you haven't done
Think about what you have done
Don't let the people from your past lower you

As I step away
I think about what they are saying
What I have achieved from my past
Has saved me for what I am about to do next

My head starts to slow
As perspective starts
I calm myself after the nervousness
I know what I have to do

The next step is about to come
To go back into the wide World again
Take a step along the road
And take the I don't care what you say

He took me on because I am good at what I do
Not because of what you say
Wait and see
You will find your confidence again Heartily

Out it all comes
It is amazing what talking to two people can do
What a new World I haven't seen before
Looks like, a step outside my comfort zone.

Friday, 16th August 2013 - Scarry or Scary Story?
#Timetotalk

Emotional scars can be so different to the ones from violence, however they can still hold the same pain, just because they aren't seen doesn't mean that they don't hurt as much and they can spread so many more scars around if they aren't healed, more emotional or even self harm scars:-

Do you have emotional scars?

Do you have the scars from violence, on the outside?

Have you ever seen someone cry, and you can't see why?

Or they have been so angry?

Or even self-harmed, and you have seen those hidden scars?

I can say yes to all of these, however I have never self harmed myself except not to take tablets or trying to kill myself, that is the only self harm I have ever done, that doesn't mean I haven't seen someone with the scars, because I have the scars that hurt inside and out.

Emotional scars can hurt just as much as the ones outside that are shown from violence. Some of us have learnt to deal with them better than others, either by clouding them over until they suddenly burst or are triggered, some of us are able to place the emotional scars so that we can deal with them and for others like myself we carry them around like a heavy burden until such time as we have found a way we can deal with them.

Just because they are not seen doesn't mean that there aren't reminders, that there won't be something either scary or even some happy memory that won't trigger these memories or a person.

For me all my emotional scars have come from different times in my life, which I haven't dealt with as I am going along, the easiest way, I have pushed them to the back of my mind and kept on going along, which is why the dark cloud started as grey and murky when I started, then as each incident happened the cloud has got darker, pushing each thing to the back so that people can't see them and I want to forget, but that is not how it works, because I could only take so much.

With each episode of my depression it has taken me over more and more. When my partner had a mental breakdown due to his emotional and violent scars, I was determined to beat mine inside without even going down the paths I had been before. I said to myself "Why should I, this is a clean, fresh new path of my life, I have to be strong now, independent enough that I can work this out without going down the depression path again, I want to beat this without changing, only being strong for me and my partner"

What I didn't realise though was that I had started there already and as my partner went down his downward spiral, I could feel myself slowly falling into the same trap, still putting the smile on for everyone, work, him, his mum and his family(my new family) at that time I didn't have anybody to say anything to except keep screaming on the inside. Even though I had been the one to walk away, I had a husband who was still messaging me and didn't get the idea of no contact, this was making things worse and getting me even more and more down into the depression. I was starting to cry in corners, where nobody could see me not even my new partner, because I wanted to show him strength by supporting him and helping his elderly, sick mum as well.

It took about five months when I finally broke down and told him what was happening to me, he sat holding me and said he realised that there was something wrong, that I had changed for a couple of months, that I had got lower and lower and more into myself, not wanting to talk. What I will say is that this is one person I never expected to realise anything was happening a) because of his own illness b) because we hadn't been together for very long, it just goes to show how well someone can know you and even now I am still amazed when he can see the difference in me and knows me so well.

My highs and lows swing from one week to the next, can also change to a very low and very pessimistic. My partner has taken my hand and walked with me every step of the way, for him it has been tiring as it was for me with his. He has given me the strength to take a new step forward each time I have wanted to, he has also allowed me to step back with hesitation, knowing that these steps back are so that I can take my steps into perspective. He has been there for me to have a shoulder to cry on when I needed it even if I couldn't tell him why.

The only reason I can say that my darkest cloud came this time because I have a new fresh start, living somewhere new, with someone who finally knows who I am, who wants to be with who I am and willing to accept me in whatever way I come, he won't push me away if I become ill he just wants me to be me.

I wish I could say that for my employers, friends or family, who think that for all the emotional scars I have, these should be put behind me and as easy as that start all over again without the pain I have inside. For this I have had to leave some of those friends behind and out of my life, this hasn't been easy, it never is, in fact at times it has been quite painful, I have made new friends along the way either online, face to face or still talking to one or two old friends.

I have learnt that I do have to smash my past to pieces and these people form my old memories, now I have to put them back together so it is easier for me to look at or talk about when I meet new people, new employers, new friends and a new comfort zone.

The only thing I ask of employers is to help with new people to settle them in, contractors or permanent, you seem to take more time over permanent staff, but, contractors need it as well, they are the ones who have to make transition from company to company, you don't have to pussyfoot, just be helpful.

The only other thing I ask is if you don't have any counselling to help your workers get some and perhaps a little training from a Mental Health Organisation to help with understanding mental health illnesses, stress, depression(whatever level), bipolar and anything else, we all want to work and there is no reason why we can't with a little help. If you get a network of people to talk to include everyone who works there not just YOUR staff, the ones that have come in from agencies as well. This is another thing that doesn't help making your temp contracts to be separated from the permanent staff. 1 in 4 people suffer from mental health illnesses and you or a member of your staff could be the next ones, I know you may think of us as replaceable perhaps, if you thought about us as irreplaceable and get some help you wouldn't need to be spending so much on replacing your staff either with temporary staff or recruiting new members of staff.

So you see throughout my contracting and permanent careers I have come against a brick wall inside and out. People who say they understand, but, don't really know because they never stop to ask the real time of day with you, the people who do not want to get to know you.

Friends who say they want to stand with you, when really all they mean is that you have depression and that is fine, I will just ignore you and it for a while until you are getting better and you are back to your normal self because, I really can't be bothered, don't believe in it or don't have time to be messing about with things like that, I will leave it to the professionals.

When it happens for you, I will be there for you, because..... I understand, I have been there and I do have the time to support you, to talk you through all your bad scars no matter what they are until the chemistry is balanced in your body again. That is a friend. Take a look around you today, do you see what is happening? Can you see someone crying? Have you stopped and asked them why or are you too busy, does it matter if you know them or not, perhaps just take a tissue out of your pocket. Talking to someone can halve this heartache, can help all the scars, it doesn't matter whether you know them or not either. If a friendly face asks you if you are alright today and they have stopped tell them because it is #Timetotalk to day to help understand stigma, without letting people think we are ashamed of it.

Tell me your story as I have told you part of mine.

My name is Susan Bell, I am 42 years old, I write to lift Stigma from Mental Health and to stop the shame of any mental health illness as it is #Timetotalk.

©Heartily Mindful

Mental illness is nothing to be ashamed of. Neither is talking about it. It's #TimetoTalk.

time-to-change.org.uk

Friday, 16th August 2013 - It is #Timetotalk with #Timetochange

Watch out, watch out I am about, talking again about talking, I love talking, I am not the greatest at it, but, I want you to understand, that unless we talk we cannot change things in this world even just a little bit, if we don't want to be ashamed or embarrassed about our mental health illnesses

There is no phrase
No saying
That can help me
Get better quicker

It takes time
It could take a small amount
Or even a long time
Sometimes even never

What I do know
Is what it will take
A lot of pain
Pain that will hurt

That pain
Will even out
Once the scars
Have healed in time

There is no money
Just my writing that keeps me
Running alongside you
To try to help others

I don't want to just help me
I want to help you
Help you stop being ashamed
Ashamed of your Mental Health Illness

Give it time
You too will feel like me
For the moment
Try helping others by talking

Talk out loud
Shout over the brick wall
The all that surrounds us all
The one that needs to be broken down

The worst pain of all
Is the misunderstandings
Of people around us
Tell them , talk to them, this is #Timetotalk

We need to help
#Timetochange
Lift all the stigma
And the embarrassment of being mentally ill

It is #Timetotalk with #Timetochange

Saturday, 17th August 2013 - Talk, Listen, Hear, because now is #TimetoTalk

I love writing and a lot of you know that writing is my way of talking to people, so please read ahead:-

Inspiration comes from the heart and the head just makes it up as the heart beats, change comes from the head and is followed along with the beats of our heart.

Sometimes I have this in both capacities, but, others I don't, so I have to go along with inspiration. Change to me inspires what I write. As you have read in other pieces I have written before, that change has happened so much in my lifetime.

A lot of change has been probably the worst things I could have ever done and if my parents were reading this now, they would want to know what I meant, I didn't follow my instincts. Now you ask "Why did you do the changes if they were for the worst?"

Because it was the path I took. As all of us have done at one time or another we have made bad decisions, but my emotional scars show they were all the wrong ones even the violent scars show that. With men who didn't care except to have or be married to someone..

It was a vicious cycle one after the other, emotional, psychological, violent as I know it is for many others of you out there too, it is hard to break, the worst thing is when friends cannot see what is happening to you until the shouting from that person starts and the threats.

I was so scared about how I was ever going to get out of it, it took me over a year to decide to walk, even then I was scared what I was going to do, I didn't know how I was ever going to do it, but, I did to change, change the life that I was living for something different.

I found new friends and new old friends, who helped me, I still have my old friends and a few new friends standing by me. Emotional scars huh?

I hear people who sit around me at work and say "so you split up from you husband" without thinking about what is inside and then proceed to laugh and tell me someone else has split up from his wife or so and so has....they laugh without knowing what the pain is inside of seeing what is happening to you, they laugh because they do not understand, they are scared to ask the details, they don't want to know as long as their lives stay the way they are which are perfect, just starting out with people or have been in their perfect marriages for ten, twenty, thirty years, the children to prove it.

It is the cause of being scared, because they don't want to hear what you are saying, don't understand, don't want to understand, they think that there is no need, yet if we talked a little bit more and understood a little bit more either by work colleagues, friends and family then couldn't we just stop the mental health illness that is starting in that person.

Talking, I know I hark on about it, but we have so lost the touch for it, since we have had email, messaging, facebook. With talking goes listening and until any one of us listens we won't hear what is being said. Someone could be crying out today for help and you aren't listening, it took me a week or so to hear my partner and to talk to him.

Last year Roger and I got together in the August, I met him only the month before and we thought we were going to be just friends, he had just moved his furniture from his old house to him mum's, where he was going to look after her as he had split from his ex-wife. His emotional scars weren't showing. My friend who had introduced us had told him to mind his back, which he was starting to show. So I could see those scars, the sad look upon his face were showing the scars from deep inside and the not knowing of what is going to happen next, I wish I could have hugged him that day, the first day I met him.

We messaged and text each other in between this and the next time we met.

When I next met him, he wasn't so low, not as that first day I met him, he was laughing with me and acting like the school child on his first date.

I wish I had watched out earlier or recognised it earlier or even heard what he was saying earlier than the few months down the line. He suffered from a very bad back which he went to the doctor and they had thought that he was starting to get depression, then I started seeing the signs, not until he had nearly broken down, I persuaded him to talk to me and then the doctor, who he was due to see for his back anyway.

So you see even I'm not perfect and I know it, but, I did hear him, I listened to what he was saying and understood that he wasn't his normal bubbly self, that it was difficult to get him motivated into things he loved doing, which was when I started going downhill, because I was helping him and helping to look after his mum as well. The only person I had was my best friend from miles away and I am not just talking 10 miles, I could visit, I mean at least 40 miles away, who was struggling herself.

I was still trying to get myself over my split and all I could think about was how everyone else was having it easy. What I realised was that Roger was now in the final stages, denying it to himself which was when we sat and talked about it, that he cried and I told him he had to see the doctor, most of his friends and my friends by this time had either gone off or were ignoring him which wasn't helping at all, because he needed to have someone other than me to talk to, but, we got through it.

He didn't want to tell anyone that he had broken down, that he had been weak, so as well as not seeing his friends normally, he had pushed them away by being scared of what they would say, there is nothing wrong with admittance of a mental health illness because it is truly a strength, it takes strength from inside to say I have a mental health illness, it is a step in the right direction to changing you.

As Roger went through the steps of getting lower and lower, I was there beside him as a friend and a girl friend mostly he would say his best friend, the one person who would hear him and nudge him in the right direction. I was there when he thought a many a time of killing himself, he often tells me that I am the one thing that kept him from doing anything stupid(killing himself he means), could you imagine how it feels to be the one person in the world that stops all this.

I could because I have been there, and I will tell you something else, he is the only reason for me.

It takes strength and courage to finally admit to the pain inside and seek help, there is no shame or weakness in mental health illnesses, that is the way it should be, it is only because of how mental health illnesses have been treated in the past that we are all scared of saying anything.

'Lock them up' it was said 'throw away the key' the words are so clear put them into an asylum, they aren't fit to be in the community, they could hurt anyone, they are all so violent.

Watch the tears roll down my cheeks, do they look like they are going to hurt you? No. I could name any amount of celebrities are they doing any damage? No in fact we all look like you human beings, we aren't animals to be kept locked up all our lives, you wouldn't have half the workforce if that was the case!! I can tell you what if you listened more to your employees more you would hear that they are needing more help.

Lives can be so complicated or busy these days that we don't take time to stop and assess where we are or what we need to talk about, we are so busy talking about somebody else instead of to them or about our own lives is there any wonder we are where we are!

We need to stop, process our thoughts and talk to someone, reach out to a friend to realise where we are going, before we get too far, to be able to help ourselves, Talk, listen, hear and if needs be help to anyone a friend, family, work colleague or a complete stranger that looks upset instead of just leaving them to think they are alone.

Nobody is alone, there is someone to help if only we reached out to help or be helped.

If you are reading this I am assuming you have a mental health illness, if not then try to understand the next person, try empathy for once instead of being scared of what they are saying, sit and hear them, send them in the right direction, dry their tears so they can think clearly, have a coffee with them.

My name is Susan Bell, I have a mental health illness, I write to help myself and those who can hear me with a mental illness, the truth is I have courage and strength to be able to do these things and I am starting to realise it. My scars will heal with pain, I have Roger by my side to help through all of this, I have broken my cycle, it has taken me a long time to realise how and to find someone who will hear me finally so I can put the scars elsewhere in my picture, so I can dance to the new music I hear and to fall in love with my soulmate.

Roger is my partner, he has had a mental breakdown, he looks after his mum as a carer and stands by me to support me and encourage me through everything.

All I ask is Talk, Listen, Hear and Talk again let it start today because now is #TimetoTalk & #TimetoChange put a pledge on their wall today.

Saturday, 17th August 2013 - Calm! - Impossible or Impassable!!

I can't keep still I have to get up and walk as I think about this poem as it is the only way
I can think, because I can't seem to sit still and the tears will not stop falling for wanting
to be calm:-

As I run through my head
Trying to find what thoughts I want to settle
I feel like I am chasing a never ending speed horse
Round and round chasing my thoughts
I wish they would stop and let me take a rest

The hustle and bustle on the street
Feels like the thoughts that I am chasing
Never ending until suddenly they come to a stop
Halt, don't go there
My head is aching from all of this and stomach churning

I feel like I have been stood still
Stood where everybody just pushes past me
With my tears falling
Not noticing what is going on
The same as me not knowing what is happening

The manic pace of what is going around
I can hardly sit still to think
I have fidgeted, agitated and still nobody notices
Nobody knows they just pass me by
Their lives are all oh so perfect

Why would they want to know
How could they want to know
Because inside my head it is just a rush
A rush I need to slow down
One I can't talk about it will just come out as waffle

I wish I could stop chopping and changing
How do I cope on with this
When I all I want to do is live normally
I want to sit down to do one thing

When all I can think about is doing many things
I look around and wonder
Why me
I listen to my music and hope it will calm
It doesn't, just keeps me sitting and fidgeting
I'm just crying because I no longer know what to do

I have to keep moving
Because I can't keep still
Even if it is my legs and my fingers
They are all moving like the thoughts in my head
STOP and Time out

Trying so hard to work with this
I am so scared

Sunday, 18th August 2013 - You Are The Stronger Person (not a poem)

What are we?

Where do we belong?

What gives other people rights to judge us?

Why do they judge us when they don't even know, don't even understand?

We are human beings who have mental health illnesses, that has to be an easy answer doesn't it or does it? The answer a lot of people who don't understand will say that we are just self-pitying, self-obsessed, selfish people who live within our past or the sadness that surrounds us giving us any excuse not to do anything except be ill, we are violent, rude, unsociable, make life harder for ourselves than it should be and couldn't care less about anybody else except ourselves that we do deserve to be locked up and to throw away the key (I am sorry, if this is harsh, however I never said it was easy either).

The other things that could be done or said, ignore, laugh, bully or avoid us. What they are doing is judging us because such as human behaviour is to be scared of unknown and what we don't understand, for some they would much rather not hear about it so choose to ignore it, others I am sorry to say will laugh, bully or avoid us because we are different, but, what we need to help them with is that we are not unknown, different or strange, we are HUMAN BEINGS too.

This is why I write because, I have had all the above, "pull your socks up all you have had is a few setbacks in life", "Leave it all in the past", "You need to forget it now, you have a new life" - can I tell you something which I suspect you already know they don't work.

All of the above is something I have heard, that is because they don't know me they choose to judge me instead of talking and understanding by what they think they know, which is nothing.

For those of you who don't understand this that has been travelling around with me for years has reared his ugly head all too often, even in times when I have been with someone who says exactly the above, someone who was totally ignorant of the fact that I was going down that road. He didn't believe in depression he thought that it was all in other people's heads and couldn't see what was right in front of his eyes, even when one

Christmas I smashed a glass with my bare hands and blood poured out, even when I started acting irrationally, with emotion and anger for no reason.

It is difficult to talk to anyone when all these judgements are made about us, I think that until those don't know or understand that we are just as normal as they are and that we have an illness as diabetes is an illness, just needs understanding the judgement will keep standing like the brick wall that is built up around us.

Most of us work for a living each and every day with the support of friends and family around us. What a lot of us are unable to tell those work colleagues is what is happening to us, because there is that brick wall, you know the one that stops us from telling anyone anything about how we feel.

Some of us have no support at all except for friends and sites online, because if there is family or friends they are judging us.

It is so sad that with the technology we have today we are still in the dark ages where people cannot or will not sit and listen to their own fellow human beings and pass judgement as soon as we say that we have a mental health illness, it is almost as bad as some years ago saying I have diabetes until it was understood. Now I know how they feel.

For those of you out there who think they will be judged by their family or friends, try it first, you never know, if not talk to any of the websites that are linked on the side of this blog site.

I wish I had something to tell you except, try to help them understand, if they shun you do not take it personally, it is because they are afraid and are scared, tell them to read up about it on numerous amount of sites, that it isn't as scary and it is better understood than it ever used to be. Be the first ones to tell them, that you need them to talk things through or even just to be there, help them to understand, show them a site whilst you are there with blogs, ones like Time to Change where you will find a list of organisations who will help you or those wanting to support you and those around you.

The only person who it should be scary for is yourself, I know because I am there, I have a family who is telling me to leave the past to the past, which I would love to do dearly and I will do one day, what they don't know is what has happened in my past to finally break me to where I am and also not knowing what has caused this mental health illness, they think without looking around them that it is all to do with the past when there are other reasons for mental illness. Some of my friends have abandoned me and Roger, there are others who are willing to stand by both of us not judging us by what we have now, but, who we are as human beings.

This I have to be thankful for. I am also thankful for Roger for understanding whatever happens to me and supporting me through this as I stood by him.

As you know the human mind is a complex piece of us, not knowing what will happen next is the scary part, you have enough people to help you and support you, you aren't alone.

This is why it is #timetochange, time to change other people's judgement and attitude towards mental health illnesses, #timetotalk about our own experiences to help others to either tread in our footsteps or to be able to send them in the right direction. As with any other illness, there is no right or wrong answer, it is the way that is easiest for you to survive and you will for a reason, even if it is to hold your head up high and say I got through it, I survived now I want to tell you how.

I am no expert, all my writing is through experience, personal experience, it doesn't have to be 20+ years as mine is, it can be just the few months, talking about it, trying to help others by taking the shame away from mental health illness or the judgement of those who are scared and don't understand helps anyone.

That is why 42,219 people to this date and time (going up all the time) pledged on the wall of #timetochange pledgewall to stop the stigma of mental health, to challenge where it is needed.

We will one day stop the discrimination, judgement and stigma of mental health allowing all of us to be able to talk about it as we can diabetes, not being ashamed to ask how we are today and what treatment we are getting.

My name is Susan Bell, I am 42 years old, I do have a mental health illness, my partner is Roger, he is 43 years old and he had a mental health breakdown, we both want to help lift the stigma of mental health illnesses, the shame, judgement with the experiences of each of our illnesses through my writing on here and in a book.

One day our society will accept us for who we are not our illness until then we just have to keep helping them understand who we are and to stop thinking that mental health illnesses are to be ashamed about by talking about it.

You are a stronger person and YES, this is my speech because it is #TimeToTalk!!

We will get there one day!

I pledge...

To challenge Mental Health stigma and discrimination
whenever I see it! I will no longer be ashamed of my own mental
illness but speak up instead. I will do my best to educate
people that are ignorant and derogatory towards Mental
Health by sharing my own experiences and those of others.

time to change
let's end mental health discrimination

~ Time To Talk :)

Sunday, 18th August 2013 - What a Day To Have Fun?

I sit here now listening to two little girls enjoying themselves in what is left of the sunshine today in the garden, with friends, I have seen steam tractors travelling down our lane as they all make their way home as I watch my fish in the pond swimming around in the new pond just dug this year, through my partner - Roger's therapy for his breakdown and his back. Our dog is banned as he scares our fish by dropping in his own unwanted animals or toys to the fish:-

As I walked down my garden
I felt the wind on my face
Wondering if I would see my fish
Hoping that they would be swimming around
Helping to give me peace

As I watched the pond
The wind swirled around quite coolly
And the sounds of the tractors chugging along
The engine and tractors of the steam rally for today
Choking the air with the smoke from their funnels

As I watched them go by
I saw the children enjoying themselves
On the trailers behind them
What fun it must be to sit on one of them
I smiled to myself

I felt the sun poking its nose through the trees
Holding every last minute of the day
As I went back to watching the fish
Swimming around the bottom of the pond
What a life it would be to swim carefree

I listen to the birds, the Wood Pigeon, Swallows as well
The hum of the insect flying around
The flowers and weeds floating in the pond too
Oh my goodness what I would give to be you
So free and easy floating around

The sun has been out
A nice cooling wind
Birds and the bees flying around the sky
As the fish swim in amongst the weeds of the pond
What a beautiful day for the children and adults to have fun at a steam fair

Tuesday, 20th August 2013 - Round And Round

I have been to my new therapist today (counsellor to some) and I have had a brain wave
this is where I want to be I know this is what I keep saying, but, a girl can dream can't
she no matter what :-

Round and round they go
What do they do
I wish that I knew
And what happened to the last one too

The thought that was there
A wish to be sane
The sanity covered
With thoughts and messes

Darkness that covers
And then goes away
The sound of silence
And the voices that won't go away

More and more it pushes me on
To do the things
And the places
I don't want to go

The spiral goes on
Until one day I fall upon
The way to climb out
Of this loopy wheel

So what do I do
And how does it happen
That is the trick
I need to find out

What triggers the things
For me getting lower
What helps me to push
Even higher

What you don't get
When it is easy to say
"Snap out of it"
That is harder than you think

Working so hard
To come out of this hole
The black monster
Has been following me all of my life

When I go low
I don't want to be here
OMG I want this to be
The last of the sessions under this black deed

One day I know
That I will walk free
If not then I know
I will manage me

The smile will be back
And I will know how to handle
The one thing that has bugged me
Like a black monster

Instead of running
I will stand still and fight
It will try laughing
But I will bite in there on it's bum

Then I will stand and cheer
Thank you all
And to those

Who got me here!!

Wednesday, 21st August 2013 - Racing Thoughts!

What a busy day, doing all sorts of things including interviews, taking photos and tidying up, I have literally just about caught my breath:

Up and down
And round and round
In and out
And down below

My thoughts have turned
Inside out
The rushing about
In this busy world

When I am calm
They will slow right down
To allow me to think
A little more clear

Whilst they do
I will write this poem
Of how my thoughts
Seem to you

They will be
A little confused
Perhaps a bit low
When all they are, are blue

Whilst I can think
So quickly
My fingers type quite rapidly
What they to you

Are they thinking
They are unsure
But, what about the score
Of the emptiness inside my head

Oh my goodness
I do seem confused
Perhaps frustrated
With the thoughts running through my head

The silence around me
Should help
But I think about the doubt
With the running and racing around

Whilst you sit here and read this clearly
I am starting to feel weary of the time
I have left around this writing
With the thoughts that won't sit still

Do not disturb
It says above my head
So I can collect what is inside

When the time comes, I will write what I can!

Thursday, 22nd August 2013 –

Soon It Will Be Saturday At Last!!

What a day at work today:-

An ode to the great fresh air
Sitting here in the soft evening breeze
With the soft evening sun just touching my fingers
And the time flying by
To somewhere, nobody knows

A day in a life of the great office worker
Come home to what you are good at
Working again at the lovely computer
As my head is full with the muddle of the day
I am wondering what is going to be install for me tomorrow

Wow, it felt good to get out there again
And step back out of the temporary comfort zone
The one I had contained myself in for several weeks
Seeing and meeting new people again
Even working at their systems for just a while

As the day whizzed by
So did my head
The stuff and nonsense
That filled with with dread
Is this all correct what I have filled there

With the nicest of people
Surrounding my desk
Training me on the most basic of stuff
My head still got through without any stress
When it got to 16.50 it was time to go home

Home, shop or home
Oh dread, the horrible shop again
It was only for a few bits and pieces
The things that you have to have
To do the tea pizzas

Where has the time gone
It is time to head home
Cook the tea
Write a piece
And then it will soon be time for my own home

Look at what I have accomplished today
Through going to work
Stepping outside of my own little comfort zone
And widening it further
I will be glad for the time to go past

Soon it will be time for Saturday at last!

Thursday, 22nd August 2013 - A Wondrous Good Night

As in my usual sign off for tonight, I leave you with this poem for a peaceful night:-

I sit in the garden on a summer's eve
Hear the birds singing
Listen to the insects
Watch the butterflies

Look around the garden
Feel the touch of the sun on my skin
The breeze blowing the clouds

The clouds that are about to blanket
Over our side of the Earth for our night
Time for all of us to sleep
First of all listen to the sounds

The twinkle of the stars in between the clouds
Where the satellites
That survey our earth
Pass by for us to be safe

Safe and sound
As they wander around
So the wrap of the Angel Wings
Feel the softness touch you

Hear the sounds
See the night lights
Watch the wondrous insects fy about
Then take a peaceful breath to sleep

Friday, 23rd August 2013 - Help Them Understand! #timetotalk

We will get ourselves heard and understood, just one brick at a time with each story we tell.

I talked today, did you?

I walked today, where were you?

I watched today go by, what happened to you?

Why must I ask the stupid questions

Because actually for a lot of us these questions are the ones we ask day in day out of the people who we know, the ones that want to stand by us, but, actually are nowhere to be found when we need them.

We want to talk and they are hiding, how many times have you heard the line from your family or friends and really they are just so scared of what we are about to tell them or they don't want to hear that we are ill.

"I have been there, come on pull your socks up I came out the other side" What they actually mean is they have been there, they never asked for help because they thought it was weak and wimpish and they think that you should stop messing around, stop being self-centred and get on with your life. Which in my line of theory is they don't understand, they are scared of what you could do or where this could lead. What you need to do is let them know that all you need is for them to be there and not lecture.

I know how difficult it is for you to even say that or to withstand the shock and judgement they have just laid upon you within the last few minutes of that conversation and how you are unable to get your breath back and tell them what you need, I know because, I can't even do it so yes I am a fine one too talk. I know a man who has though.

Roger, my partner sat on the phone and talked to my friend a very good friend who didn't understand why I was pushing people, friends a way, you see for me it is a security thing, I push before they push me and walk away, but, she couldn't get this, because people including my family have been walking away from me and leaving me alone for the whole of my life I have learnt to end things before I let them finish, it is a security thing so I don't get hurt. The last time was in my second marriage so I have always tried to end things with others.

As he sat and talked to her, she said she understood, she saw me one Sunday on a good day oh nearly six months ago and I haven't seen her since, what she thought was I was alright, there was nothing wrong because she found me on a good day, I put a smile on my face and cried when I got home and boy didn't I go low that week.

I have learnt since then that there are some who will say anything to keep you as a friend even to believe what you say, but it is what they do after, perhaps this is my insecurity of making friends I am scared of rejection, I know that everyone is rejected, to worst of all is being rejected or pushed away when you are ill especially with a mental health illness, one you have been strong enough to be open and honest with your friends about.

I would start by talking to them, gathering as much information about what your mental illness is and how it is going to affect you. Talk to your doctor, talk to a mental health practitioner, perhaps they maybe able to give you some advice, take down some names of websites.

Help them to understand that this is not just a phase, it is not just in your head, that you are ill and you need some help even if it is someone to talk to, you aren't alone, there are others in a similar situation who have friends or family who can't understand even work colleagues.

Today, I spoke for the first time about how I had gone down the path after Roger had, pulled him through it and got myself into the dark cloud as well, but, am finally learning to manage this, I have worked all the way through, I have still brought in some money, bought some nice things even extravagant to me, what others may call normal. I have started work again now as well, but, for an understanding manager, someone who smiled when I said I write for mental health.

I want to be able to tell you how good it is to start feel or think as though I am managing it enough to work with it and to be able to tell someone that I have been down that road only as recent as this year, he said that mental health is not spoken about.

The one thing I will say is respect whichever practitioner you use, because they are so undervalued, if you think how hard it is to qualify and to help someone who has illnesses like ours, think about it the next time you are about to shout at them or disrespect them, it has to be a very hard profession especially as mental health illnesses are thought basically as crazy people.

We are not crazy, we are people who have an illness in our heads, something you cannot see, we are not to be laughed at, sneered at or shouted at, we are not self centred, or stupid or thick we are ill, chemically imbalanced, the next time you hear it challenge it, help them to understand that a lot of us want to work with it, we just do not get help.

If there was more assistance in the workplace then maybe just maybe more of us would be working and the government would not need to pay more benefits and if there was more understanding a lot of us would go back to work. One brick at a time and we will get there, we will get more understanding from people whom are around us, be it loved ones, family, friends or work colleagues.

Let's start in an easy place and take the first brick down to telling our stories. My name is Susan Bell, I am 42 years old, I have been suffering with mental health illnesses for over 20 years and this time I am determined to either beat it or manage it. I have supported my partner, Roger who is 43 through his mental health breakdown and he has come out of the other side.

We have struggled, but, we know that we will get there. There is more to do today, so it is #timetotalk and #timetochange other people's perception of mental health and tell them who you are with a willingness to talk about it to lift the stigma through, friends, family and work places.

I have told you who I am now tell me your story and who you are, just write on the pledgewall where 42,848 other people have written on there before to this day.

Thank you for listening and reading.

Saturday, 24th August, 2013 - Watch The Sunshine

(Not a Poem)

Can you hear the rain falling even though it is sunny outside?

Can you see the darkness even though the sun is shining brightly with a blue sky?

Can you feel the icy cold even though it is boiling hot?

Can you hear the roar of a monster with the silence ringing in your ears whilst everyone is chatting away around you.

The rain is the tears in you and rolling down your cheeks as the sun shines through your windows from behind your dark curtains. You feel the pain that hurts, it is almost as though someone has taken your whole World away, when in fact it is still there, it is waiting for you to look outside in.

As you sit on the floor, bed, in a corner, settee thinking about why you are crying, watching the memories from the past that are too painful to usually remember, except this time they had been pushed to the back and are now playing a part in your illness, a part that you never thought it would play, you were hoping it had gone away, it hasn't. Your past is now playing a part in your present as it is in mine.

I am going to let you into a secret though, something I have never wanted to tell the world about, except this year things have changed, I want to tell you that I am here because of my past and I want to say thank you, for those who have played a part don't start pulling down your jackets and start feeling proud of yourselves because it isn't all to be proud of, most of my past has been like living a nightmare, marriage rape, violent and emotional abuse is nothing to be proud of just to get your own way.

The reason I am saying thank you is so that I can talk to those who are listening to me now, so they can learn from my mental health illness and your ignorance and to show my readers that the past can teach you or guide you down the right path for the future and the present.

One lesson I have learnt is the man I love over and over again and more than words can say, if anything that was the best start. I learnt to write again, write not just books or poems, write for the good of others as well as myself. I love writing it has helped me in so many ways and I hope it helps others, there is no way of changing this, I have learnt to love photography and walk with nature, watch birds.

The other lesson I have learnt is supporting each other and learning to listen, talk and hear to actually be best friends. There is no-one controlling me, they are just loving me and taking care of me.

What it takes is for you to turn the picture you have as a bad memory and piecing it together so that you can learn from it, help you to take a perspective on how you want your future to be, perhaps changing it if you can without too much pain. To take the music you used to dance to and put it in a place where you are able to play it again, there is so much I won't listen to still because I still feel the pain from my past and that hurts.

For me to sing karaoke with knowing that I can and someone isn't going to scream and shout at me for doing it (I used to sing solos in church and learnt to sing at school). It was because I had someone who didn't want me to enjoy myself. You see what I did last year was smashed that memory and started to put it back together in the picture of my future and present so I could look at it and think I sang, I was nervous, but, I sang. When asked why didn't I sing whatever I wanted I just shrugged my shoulders and the story above was why, the one thing that helped me was that I got others singing and I got applauded for singing last year, helping the party go with a swing, so I replaced my old memory with a new by putting the pieces in my picture frame, where I can look at it.

Me loving someone and feeling secure without pushing him away, it has been awhile since I have done that, since the discussions we have had for me to push him away to feel the insecurity that he is going to leave me alone, he has shown me that he is going nowhere, that I can be my own person unlike I have been before, I can wear fun t-shirts, that I can look good without looking dowdy.

You see having a life that has had no sunshine, a black cloud covering it and then you walk into the bright sunshine you suddenly walk back into the shade, which is where you should be and you shouldn't you deserve to shine as much as anyone else does, step out into the light sometime and take a look around, take a friend with you and talk about why you have been sat in your corner, under your duvet, stuck behind the brick wall, because there is nothing like it.

Roger is not the only friend I have that has helped me and started to understand me, I have learnt not to push my best girlfriend away and she has needed me as well as I need her to talk to, sometimes I find it difficult, there was a time I used to sit on Facebook and chat for hours, there are only two people I have talked to a lot and a few I have started to. Julie I have known for nearly 28 years in fact it is 28 years this year, we have gone through so much together and we will carry on supporting each other through everything. The one thing I would like to say to her is I love you as a very very good best friend, always there to talk to and I love you very much for being there, thank you.

You see I have made new friends spread across the internet from writers, patient Leader and others who I can say I have sent my posts to and others I have message personally, who have helped me to step out of one comfort zone into a wider one, my new pathway will continue until I have got to where I want to be and that is not where I am.

I know as you will that there will be some steps back, never take them as backward steps, but, resting to take perspective of your life of where you are now as I have so often been advised, so in the meantime I will write and keep on writing until my head has stopped, which will never happen believe me.

Every step you take needs to be baby steps, because it doesn't matter how small, it is a step forward and you may need to stop, that is fine. The other I say is remember to keep talking as you make each step, it doesn't matter how, just talk to someone, this is all I say and I am not screaming and shouting about it today.

Stand up, walk to a mirror and look at yourself, you may hate yourself, but you are beautiful, inside and out, you are amazingly strong and you don't realise it, if you have been to your doctors you know you are. There are only three things that could call me strong, support my new partner, Roger through his breakdown, admit that I was mentally ill and look at my job and realise that I need time out from it.

You, have done at least one of these because otherwise you wouldn't be sat here reading me waffle, you are strong, you are beautiful and you are awesome you will see it in the mirror one day and you will feel it, because you will learn to love you when your past has been put in the frame behind the mirror you are looking in.

You will learn a new dance to a new piece of music which is more suited to you and one by one you will learn a new step into your new future, the music will change along the way, but, you will be able to look back and hear the old with the realisation that is the last time you hear it because you don't need it anymore as will some of the old memories do the same.

I end this piece with a plea for you to find someone to talk to as I have over the years, to clear the monster, so you can see the sunshine, so you can hear the music and the speech around you instead of the silence or the monster's roar. I haven't yet, but, I am getting there one small step at a time and I will carry on with support and talk.

My name is Susan Bell, I am 42 years old I am a mental health illness sufferer and so was my partner Roger, 43 years old. We both stand for #Timetotalk, we have both pledged on #Timetochange pledgewall, we want to help lift the stigma with friends, workplace and family also with anyone who doesn't understand, we want to help them understand.

Sunday, 25th August 2013 - Please Understand (not a poem)

For what we understand :-

Time, such an important concept to all of us. There are some it feels like it was only just yesterday and it is getting away from us quickly, whereas there are others who think it is dragging because we are stuck in a never ending time zone.

That is the worst feeling being stuck in the time zone that will never end, the one where yesterday keeps hitting us, where the past doesn't want to go away the bad past if you will, the memory of what happened in yesteryear.

For those of you who think I am just sitting here and writing this with no conceivable knowledge of what you are going through, you are so very wrong, I have been there and for myself I am just starting to be able to realise that I am thankful for my past, because I wouldn't be where I am now.

Yes, I know you have heard this so many times before, be thankful for your past it has put you on the path today, well this time it is right and do you know I am not the only person who is thankful for this I have an on-line friend who is probably thankful, we have started our lives a fresh, completely new. We don't see the World with the rose tinted glasses we used to but have learnt to love music and the men we are with in a new, fresh, secure way.

Those men, are our best friends, supporters and if you want our teachers. These people have been strong enough to show us that they are nothing like our past, they have helped us to be able to slowly see that we can start to put our past behind us.

I have started to be able to hear music in a different way, some I have put to the back of my head, but I am now starting to be able to watch it. My teacher has taught me to be fun, not just to be so serious (except these pieces), encouraged me to be me, that is a friend someone who will accept you the way you are.

I have never done this in my life, just doing what I want to do, working where I want to work, not always doing what somebody else wants me to do, starting a new career and it doesn't matter what I do, because this is my life, I am in control of my life, no matter how much I feel like I am spiralling, with racing thoughts.

I have been accepted by people for me and with my Mental health illness, I AM NOT my mental health illness, I am me.

You see to accept my past will be a start in the right direction a help to control some of my illness, I am the first to admit that it is not going to completely cure me, I know that there are other things that I need to help me, because there is no complete cure of it.

What has helped me is talking about it, no matter how painful and now matter how low I have gone. I know it is not the easiest thing to do, but, it helps and it has helped me and others who have gone through mental illness, to talk to someone who understands and is not scared of what or who we are.

We are not our illnesses, we have a mental illness which is hidden inside and we want to be able to talk about them instead of being ashamed.

After all, why should we be ashamed?   Why do we have to keep quiet? Because you want to hide away and not realise that we are real, that you are perfect and you couldn't care less, you think we are self-obsessed, and that your judgement is the be all and end all?

No, to all of the above questions. We should not be judged, just because you want to or you do not understand, because the fear underneath of the unknown. If you sit and listen you will know what it is, it isn't just what I have written about above, we have a chemical imbalance as a diabetic does with an insulin imbalance, do you run away scared from them, no you do not, you sit and listen and help them. This is all we need, sit, listen and understand our illnesses.

We are not mad, we are not crazy, we are normal people with a mental health illness who struggle to be heard and listened to by our friends, family and work colleagues, we want to stand up and be counted, we do not want to be ashamed of our illnesses or our past, but, there are so many people who are scared, who laugh and don't understand that we are.

This is why I started to write this blog to be heard and for others to be heard, to help me and to help others, too write for mental health. I will keep writing day by day until finally that Mental Health Illness is heard and understood as the one thing that can hit anybody at anytime in any form.

We want to be able to work, we are so scared of telling anyone it actually makes our illness worse unless we can control it any way. We are asking for the first steps to help us either stay in work or to get into work, by letting others understand and having someone to be able to talk to or managers to talk about it. We don't need to be put on the edge of the group or the centre, we want to be treated as normal.

Friends and family, stand by your loved ones all they ask is for someone to hear their cries for help, to listen to what they want to talk about, take some time out from your busy lives and try to understand the feelings of that one person you love, don't ignore them, don't be scared. If they stand you up for a tea or coffee out somewhere, don't be angry with them or take it personally, it is difficult, phone them see how they are and I mean really are, what level they are on and go and see them. Going out is not always an easy thing.

If you want them to come out, go around and pick them up, they may want to go, but, the first step out the door is not always the easiest, it is a little easier with someone. I know I have been there and sometimes I still feel the same.

I am not going to say much more except I am not a mental health practitioner, all my writings are through experience, long hard 20 years of experience with people who did not understand, some who still do not understand or want to think they have someone who is mentally ill in their family or ring of friends, it has taken me until now to find the first part of this writing my teacher, friend and someone who loves me for me not thinking about me being ill.

My name is Susan Bell, I am 42 years old, I am a writer who has a mental health illness with a partner who is 43 and has suffered a mental health breakdown. We shout out about mental illness to bring the stigma down through our own experiences, I write and he lets me write about his research. We love each other for who we are not for what we had or have.

Mental illness is nothing to be ashamed of. Neither is talking about it. It's #TimetoTalk.

time-to-change.org.uk

Sunday, 25th August 2013 - My Life Is Changing!

With a poem in my head I just sit and write:-

The wind blowing
A cool chill down my spine
As though I had been here before
Even though I haven't

I walk a little further on
To think past it
To feel the sun
That is trying to open the clouds

The Clouds that cover the blue sky
To make the day
A lot brighter
And the wind a lot lighter

As I watch on towards the trees
Where the birds are flying
With the butterflies
Flying from flower to flower

The Edge of my thoughts
They try to stand still
To stop moving around
As I sit down in the garden

Feel the bees buzzing past
I can hear them
Can' see them
Want to watch them in the flowers

Looking at beyond
Watching further on
Down the path
That has been made for me

Is it truly where I am going
Where I am wandering

How do I know what mistakes
When do I know things are right
By all my experiences
All the bad past experiences
Mistakes come with life
All you will know is that soon they will be right

The lessons we learn
Are the ones that help us take the path we are on
Take the time to gather perspective
Of why I am sat in the garden.

The music I hear
A dance I am about to learn
Is the life I am going to lead
The bumps in the road will just be there

My life is changing!

Sunday, 25th August 2013 - Hope!!

How I see my hope:-

As time goes by
So do I
So does the hope
Because I am too small

I have always hoped to do things
That matter to me
When I have got the chance
I realise that I am too small

The World passes me by
So does the time
My voice is too quiet
And the face is too small

I am lost in a crowd
A crowd of swarming people
With louder voices
Who can't hear someone too small

I am one person
I can only speak in this way
Nobody will hear me
I am too small for this world

What difference will I make
When will I make it
I don't want to give up
But I know that I am too small

I want hope to give me my life back
Give me a chance to show who I am
Tell me I am right

That my voice is loud enough to be heard and I am not too small

Monday, 26th August 2013 - Sounds All Too Familiar?

I am a little angry, but, I have no place to say anything, I want my new family to be together, unfortunately there is one who will not gel with everyone and sits in their own world, to some it sounds a little too familiar:-

As yellow as the sun
Blue like the wind
Black as the rain
White as the snow

These are the colours
My thought change to
When I can't stop in time
To calm down

Thoughts are racing
Because of something
I have been thinking
Yet have no real reason to say about

My colour today is black
Even though it is yellow and blue outside
The reason for this is the stress
Of dealing with family

This time I have no place
No place to say anything
So I have decided to write
Write about the pain inside

How the family have hurt my family
Hurt my partner's mum
Hurt him
And hurt me

I will leave it with him
As it is his family
I know that things will be left undone
I have no place to say anything

The sooner they are here
The sooner they are gone
We all know they will not stay long
As they have no time for us

They are some more who think
Think they understand
But don't, because they do not realise
That deep down there is more to life

That family is important
To stand by
To support,
To talk to.

Friends are important
So are work colleagues
Even though I am biting my tongue
My partner needs his sister to talk to

I wish she knew how much
I wish she understood
How much help he needs
Not just him, but, his mum too

One day she will find out
That day I hope will not come too late
I hope upon hope she will realise
That there are others outside of her own World

Monday, 26th August 2013 - Something...Happened!

This is how we shouldn't deal with things, but, we do if you see anyone distressed take the time to talk to them, it would help in the long run, better now than later or you will realise that things will never get better :-

Something happened a long time ago
Something I have never talked about
Something I have kept at the back of my mind
Something I want to talk about

Something happened not so long ago
Something I never spoke about
Something locked in the back of my mind
Something I will talk about

Something happened yesterday
Something I didn't talk about
Something I have put away in my mind
Something so I won't talk about

Something happened today
Something I haven't talked about
Something I am trying to lock away in my mind
Something I would talk about

So if I had talked about
The long time ago
What would have happened
Would it have been any easier

If someone had stopped to listen
If I would have stopped to talk
If someone had stopped to understand
Perhaps I wouldn't be here now

I could have unlocked it
Could have found the key
The Key to unlock the pain
Pain I have hidden for so long

How I want to talk
But, there is so much going on
So much racing through my mind
Look at it like a stormy wind

I don't know where to turn
Not sure who will want to listen
Who will understand
What, where, why and when?

I am going to sit here
I will wait
I know I need to help me though
I can't sit under the darkness

Talk to a friend
Talk to a practitioner
Talk to family
It is time for me to talk to someone!

Tuesday, 27th August 2013 - Stop this bullying!!

Take a look at something that happened to me only yesterday, it is not just happening to me it is happening to someone somewhere, at school, work or home even:-

What a whirlwind
And how could you do it
You badger and badger me
Putting me into a corner

Not letting me have a chance to say a word
Shouting at me as if I was a child
I am an adult
And I do live here

Give me the respect I deserve
Why are you doing this to me
It isn't me you need to talk to
Not me you need to shout at

Talk to the person who talked to you first
But, you haven't got the courage
You cannot stand up to them
You know that what you are doing is wrong

Stop it stop bullying me
Speak to the person who started this
I am nothing to do with this
I sit here and shut up as you push me around with your words

When you stop I walk off upstairs
I start to cry
You walk outside
And start to bully someone else

Can you not do anything except bully
Are incapable of listening to anyone
Can't you just discuss instead of hating
Or see things outside of your own little world

Dream, because you will never get anything else
You can only push around those who you know are easy targets
You don't dare take on anyone else
I look at you now and feel sorry for you

You are the sort of person
I thank goodness I haven't turned into
I will be a stronger person
And one day will fight back

When I walked up those stairs I cried
Just cried my heart out
Now I realise that I will be a better person than you
No, I am a better person than you

I have love
Care
Respect
And most of all I don't bully

I can talk about it
I will talk about
I will become a better person
In fact I am a stronger and better person that you

Because I do not need to shout at those who are unable to fight back!!!

Wednesday, 28th August 2013 - Comes At A Price!!

With school starting next week, there is so much bullying that is going to start and I know that others have already started school, there is bullying throughout work and families and I know of all people as it only happened to me on Monday and I cannot get it out of my mind:-

Stop what you are doing
Think before you do anymore
Do you know how this is going to affect this person
Or even how it is going to affect those around them
Do you know what you are even doing?

Stop! Why are you doing that
Tormenting and pestering them
Hurting all that is good inside them
Because you haven't go it yourself
Do know why you are even doing it?

It is because you are so small
Small minded not to be able to pick on
Someone who is bigger than you
A person that will give as good as you get
You won't feel good for this

Stop what you are saying
Can you not see the pain inside
Do you not know what you are saying
Because you cannot stand up and mouth off
To someone your own size

Stop being so spiteful or laughing at them
Stop pulling their hair or hitting them
Just because they have something you haven't
Stop right now
And they will see someone

Stop here comes the person you don't want to see
Someone who is bigger than you
A person that can do something to put a stop to all this
They have talked about it

Or someone who has witnessed it they have told them you are a bully!!

Don't do anymore
The harm is done
Look how they are
You have stopped them from enjoying themselves
You sad bully, what have you done!

Now take a look in the mirror
Can you see the bigger person
I don't think so
You are just a nobody
A nobody known as a bully

One day and I hope it doesn't come
You will know how it feels
I have been there
I have felt the compass pricks in my back
I have had the name calling and the pulling of my hair

I have even had the pushed into a corner
I have been bullied by family
You see I am writing and talking about it
That bully has got what she wanted
But, one day she will come across someone stronger

I hate bullies!!!!
They play mind games
They affect your mental health
And can scar you for life

Remember all this before you start next time

Thursday, 29th August 2013 - Stop Bullying Wherever!!

I would like to tell you another story of mine for bullying to help others understand that bullying is not allowed! :-

This is how I have paid
I lost friends because you thought me bad
Peer pressure harms you
It harms your self-esteem
As you get further and further down

You never saw me
You only saw what you thought of me
What you thought you could do to me
You hurt me and have harmed me
I have always thought that people hated me

I am starting to realise
What you have done
You didn't have the guts to stand up against
Someone who was stronger
Just someone you knew you could bully

Until one day I could take no more of it
I stood up and told my teacher
Told him what you had done and were doing to me
Even that day when you knew you hurt me
You got your friends to stab me in the back with a compass

My mum then showed you when she saw the marks
So I had a few friends who helped me to the teacher
And my mum took me up to the school
The headmaster was shown the same day
And saw what you had done

You see what you did and I did were to different strengths
You couldn't get what you wanted
My strength was to say to someone and to talk
To show them I was the better person
You were then suspended and taught the fearful lesson of not to do it again!

Thankfully I never saw you again

What I am trying to say is though
Whoever might be bullied needs to talk
If you don't talk about it
You will hold it in for the rest of your life and may be someone else

There are so many places to talk
Talk to your friends
Don't hold it in
There is too much around
We need to put a stop to bullying!!

Stop the tears and the pain!
Stop the bullying campaign!!

Join mine for the week - read my poems

Thursday, 29th August 2013 - My Human Angel

I am having one of my romantic moments again for the one person in the whole of this World who understands me, the one person, who is there when I fall and has stopped a many stupid moment in the past 6 months :-

For every step you take
I will be with you
By your side
Until it is shaken

For every time you stumble
I will hold you
Pick you up
Until you are steady

For every fall you make
I will hold my hand out to you
So that you can get back up
And start to walk again

For every black cloud you have
I will shine the sun your way
So that you can see the light
Until the darkness has gone

For every new path you take
I will wander down it with you
So that I can guide you
Even when you can walk alone

I will never leave you
Will always hold you
And guide you
Because of the love I have in my heart for you

Friday 30th August 2013 - Talk About It All!!

This I have written for a friend, a new friend to me and an old friend to my partner, but, we all need to talk, I have also written this for an old friend of mine and a new friend of my partner's so you see it works for all of us in each and every way and it is written for us to talk more about what is happening to us take a look deep inside you know you need to talk about all of it:-

I have walked a thousand miles
If not a million or two
By the time you have finished
I will have done more
You won't stop me

I have chatted a few million words
If to a billion or two
By the time you have finished
I will have said oh so much more
You won't stop me

A scratch, a name or even a scar
Will not stop me from saying
What I need to say
It won't stop me from doing
What I need to do

The path so far through my life
Through our lives have been long
But nothing will stop any of us
Walking through our lives
We have so much to give

The answers are somewhere
We need to keep looking
The corners may be straight
And the straight may be curved
But after all that is life

The clouds that follow
Will slowly dissipate
The sun in our skies will shine

So you see they can do all they want
You are the stronger person

You may need to talk about it
So they can't hurt anyone else
It doesn't matter what
It doesn't matter why
And for you it doesn't matter who you talk to

You are the hero
Don't give them the chance to shine
Only you
You are the one who is shining
No longer crying, it is you who has won.

Talk about it all

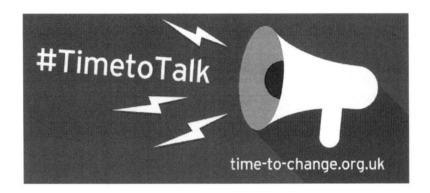

Saturday, 31st August 2013 - It Is Important To Try To Talk!

I don't think I have much to add except read, retweet, share and repost it is as impportnat as ll my other pieces at the end of the week on bullying for me:-

Have you ever felt excluded from a group because someone doesn't like the way you talk?

They are jealous that you have been to a posh school?

That you aren't the same as them and they don't want you to be, they would much rather you were sat out on your own?

They laugh at you because you do things differently?
Have you been pushed into a corner by someone who won't let you go, because you are easy to pick on and talk to someone who will give them a good fight.?

You say it is easy for me to sit here and talk about it, because it has never happened to me? Bullying can take so many forms and I have had it all my life, last year was the first year I finally broke from it where I was me, I did what I wanted not because somebody told me to or someone was the favourite so it was easier to go away.

That is how I have always been made to feel, it was easier to go away than to make myself included until now. I have a family who have made me or make me feel included until last Monday and felt like pushed out on the edge again and pulled back in.

There are times in life we will all have this. I suppose the worst thing is when you feel like you are pushed in a corner and everyone ignoring, they all wonder around with their heads looking at someone else, you carry on your own way, you are the one who ends up helping to see if this helps you to get yourself noticed, but, all that can be done is a turn in disgust when you didn't do well, or even your exams turned sour because you had been trying so hard to fit into your family and your brother who has turned all heads anyway comes out with the brownie points.

With the stress of trying to do exams from the age of 15 you had been bullied even more, your hair pulled, you were basically called dirty, your accent is posh still from boarding school and you would stay the goody goody, I can't remember the real reason except I wore my hair up a lot and told I had fleas and you were overweight. I tried to work hard, I was bubbly and friendly, but, bullied.

I got shouted at in my biology class, called names wherever I went and my geography class had to be the worst one afternoon after myself and two friends had gone to my biology teacher to tell him what was happening, I found out it was because I was laughing with some friends whilst another of my class colleagues behind me was having a fit, neither me nor my friends had seen this or heard until there was total silence, this girl and one of her friends were the ones who helped me go to my teacher, she knew even though she was having the fit, she had seen me start my laughing with my friends on the table in front of her.

My Geography class the afternoon we went to the teacher, I got stabbed in the back many times by a boy behind me, it hurt, I had to sit through the lesson with little blood spots on my shirt. I got off the coach, walked home, it was one of the afternoons my mum had come home early, I got in and started to take my blouse off in front of her, I can only remember the reason as she was talking to me about something, she then saw my back, I hadn't told her that I was being bullied.

She asked me who did it and then phoned the headmaster straight away not leaving the bullying alone, I was crying when I sat in the office and I can remember my mum and the head talking about it and how he had a report from the biology teacher about the bullying and how it all started. A couple of days later I heard that the pupil had been suspended for bullying, I never saw her again.

What I am trying to say is that no matter what you are feeling you need to talk to someone even if it isn't your mum or dad or parents, carers etc.. Talking to someone helps, I know for a little it hurts, boy does it, I am no psychology expert or mental health practitioner, I am an expert in experience.

Bullying can come in many different forms, I would never end my piece if I went through everything.

The places that are the worst are home, family, school, internet and work there are lots lots more and as I said it would never end

At the moment because of schools going back I am remembering my own worst scenario and mine isn't even the worst and I haven't told you the whole of it only the part I want you to see or the part my memory will allow me.

It cannot go on wherever the bullying takes place, in the workplace it is gossip especially gossip that is untrue and means you are laughing about someone, making them the laughing stock and making it awkward to come into work, I have been there many a time as well, I think some of us have, the problem with this is that if your home life isn't great either it can make you feel the lowest of the low, you aren't sure who to turn to or trust, believe me your doctor is the first place to be able to talk to or even a very good friend, they will sit and hear you or even family, talk to them.

I know I go on about talking, if I had done that in the beginning I wouldn't be in this position now trying to place the pieces so I can look at them without feeling emotional about them.

Bullying can do so much to someone's confidence and self-esteem as I said I know from my story above, it has taken me many years to realise that there is something more to me that what I have been in the past. That there are people who care, there are forums that are safe enough to join where they will not stand for judgement or bullying of yourself, you can be you, no matter what mood.
The mind is a very precarious place it can break at any moment if we do not take care of it or push too much information to the corner and let it all of a sudden explode.

All Mental health illnesses are chemistry imbalances, but, something pushes it and suddenly everything from our past becomes what we think is our current life, it isn't if we can reach out and talk to someone to pour hearts out to a friend it would help us and they will encourage us on to the next step.

I am also asking for those around us to understand and make people feel included, no matter what age, notice any changes in those around us and if they need our help any signs of stress, no matter how small or tall they are, if they are young or old, because we can all fall victim to bullies more so in private, notice markings like bruises or crying and talk to them. visit my most like links down the side of my blog.

I want to stop this bullying to stop the anxiety and social exclusion of others, stress that can cause people to be on their own. humans are not lonesome people we all want someone to be with even if it is a friend.

So the next time you see someone alone sit and talk to them, reach out they may need someone to talk to be a friend not a bully include them not exclude them, you never know what will happen.

My name is Susie Bell, I am 42 years old and I too have been bullied at school, work and home, I have had depression on and off for 20 years + and I am hoping that I will be able to help you and support you.

If you want to leave an anonymous comment about bullying, or just need to say something just leave an anonymous comment.

Because it is #timetotalk and #timetochange stand up to the bullies, stop your mental health illness in the future, be strong and talk to someone, it isn't easy, Childsline are a freephone number and online to talk to if you have nobody else.

Good luck for the new school year for all of you reading this and are going back to college, school or university don't hold it in talk about it.

Thank you all for reading.

Sunday, 1st September 2013 - Calm Yourself

I want to help you understand what can get you through hopelessness :

I have sat with my legs tucked under my arms
Cried when it is sunny outside
Held myself and rocked me to sleep
Called out to want to hold my loved one tight
It doesn't help

I sat on a lumpy bumpy road
After falling down
When the fall came hard
As if someone took my safety blanket from under my feet
It hurt so did the pain

At each turn of the old road
I have had someone to pick me up
Hold me
And dry the tears
No matter what they stand by me

When the silence has hurt
It has been so deftly
That I can't even hear myself
Just the voice
One voice whispers a word in my ear

This is what happens when you are strong enough
To admit there is something wrong
And that you know you need help
Someone else will be by your side

They will be the ones to calm you

Monday, 2nd September 2013 - Don't I know it!!

Well, if I could tell you I want to cry because you wouldn't believe how nice my new temporary place of work are about my depression, I think you will understand, why from my poem, please share the thoughts of my day with me:

If only all my assignments had been as nice as this
I have talked not about all my past
But enough to help me
And for others to understand I am not a moody person

I blurted enough out today
To put anyone off
But, still nobody minded
Still they kept on listening and hearing me

When I turned to say I have counselling tomorrow
Nobody batted an eye
In fact they told me it was good for me
We all sat and talked about mental health

I have not felt this relaxed and happy at work
For a very long time
I have started to feel a little more confident
I would say that I have started to let go

I am learning to laugh at me
But, there is still a long way to go
I know that my strength is coming from last week
When I went the wrong way

Since then I have gone from strength to strength
My road is long
There will be a lot of falls and rises
But, I know that is what life is all about

I will face my past
I will one day be able to turn around to face it
And say thank you with a smile
At the moment I can just say thank you

I know it will be for the strength
That my colleagues have given me
Told me what a lovely person I am
What a laugh I can be

Along the way I have picked up strengths
Strength to carry on
Thank goodness I didn't carry on last Monday
Thank you my Angel for stopping my pain in time

Because if it hadn't been for you
I wouldn't have been writing
My other Angel would have been finishing my blog
Thank you I can turn, I will smile

I am a beautiful woman, I just can't accept it yet
I am stronger than I think, I am just starting to learn it
I am not hopeless or worthless because I wouldn't have so many people who care
I will love myself as my friends love me

Can I tell you something
Let me whisper in your ear
Something very softly
IT IS TIME TO TALK BECAUSE IT IS GOOD TO TALK!!!

Don't I know it!!

Tuesday, 3rd September 2013 - I Am Always There For You!

Yes, this is a little soppy tonight and for those who aren't in the mood for it, I am only going to apologise, but, please still read it because you never know how much it will help you, This is for someone special, but, also for everyone:-

I have gone through the twists and turns
Also been on the bumps and falls
At the end of it
It was only you

There has been darkness
So many times
There have been tears
You have been my umbrella

As I walk through the rough parts
I have you to guide me
We will hold each others hands
And walk the path we want to

It is the path we want
Not what anybody wants for us
A pathway which will bring us
To our bright future

We will walk
We have so many angels around us
We have friends to support us
Most of all we have each other

I have loved you since the day I met you
Since the sun shone through the kitchen window
When you first talked to me
Because you are a beautiful man

My life wouldn't be where it is
If it wasn't for you
With the support of friends and new colleagues
My life has become complete no matter how short the time

Where I have been before
I have to put behind me
But I have to remember what I have ahead of me
And I have you with me in my future

In my life ahead
We will take walks on the beach
We will swim in the sea
We will love each other to the end

The one and only thing I wish for
Is to make both of us well enough
I know we are and will be strong enough
To stand together

I will be there as you are with me
All I ask is you talk to me
As I say to everyone else
Because now is still the #timetotalk to me

I am always here for you!

Wednesday, 4th September 2013 –

Lift the stigma from Mental Health Illness!!

Well, I just cannot believe how hard I work and still get support in talking to people, this doesn't always happen and we all need to stand together to fight the stigma for mental health, because I would say I am in the right place at the moment in my lifetime to get out of the depression I have been in for way too long :-

If you would believe what I have heard
Have you heard it anywhere around
There is support for us crazy ones
You know the ones who have lost their nut
Have their screws loose in the head

If you could believe what I have read
Have you read it at all
That there is somewhere to go
For those of us who should be in the nut house
And should be locked up away from society

I can hear the silence
I can feel the scorn
I can see the pressure
Without form
If you want to know, shout it out loud

The last two weeks have been a dream
As you wouldn't believe
I finally feel like I am getting somewhere
At the beginning of my journey
New friends, new colleagues with support

I have sat chatting and nobody minds
In fact they are more into
Talk if you feel you need to
Don't bottle it all up
You have to talk

Where is all this coming from
I have never had such a gesture
Nobody minds hearing about my depression
They want to know if I am feeling good
They also don't mind hearing I am on a low

As long as put my hours into my work
I work hard enough along with the chatter
The whole day goes along in such a clatter
Where this time has gone
I wouldn't know

It is obviously that I am enjoying my work
It is a very long time since I can say that
This is how it should be for everyone
With their own support network

If only employers would listen to my manager
They wouldn't have so many people leaving
Leaving because of mental illness
Who do you turn to
Where do you go

I know where I can go now
Do you?
If you don't you need to raise
The awareness of the illness
Lift the stigma from Mental Health Illness!!

Thursday, 5th September 2013 - I Am There!!

Whatever you do, wherever you go, I will be there because you can turn on the computer and read any one of my poems and I will be there, it hurts when people don't realise quite how much it means to see someone's writing or even to write of others:-

If I could give you what you dreamed of
What would it be?
How long would it take
Where would you go?

I know if only the silence would stop
If only the shouting would go
Only if there could be peace
Let all of us live along with each other

Let the turmoil stop
And the sun keep shining
The clouds stop shadowing
With the rain falling

Let the talking stop
Talk in front of me
Not behind me
So that I can join in

Most of all to knock the brick wall down
The one that surrounds us
The one that makes us think we are no good
When all you want to see is a beautiful reflection

There is one, stand in front of the mirror
Go on, walk up to it
Stand there and see what I see
One amazingly beautiful person

Stand up, straighten up
See the beauty inside
And the strength all around glowing
Watch the confidence and beauty grow on the outside too

Thank the past for making you what you are
Your beauty shines from it
The path long and twisting
Where the future is your own

You past is behind you
I am in front
I walk with you by your side
Holding your hand

I now stand in front of you
Where the brick wall once stood
Encouraging you out into the World
To talk about what has been inside

As I encourage you out
You will find all your friends
The ones who want to stand with you and me
By our sides

These friends of yours and mine
All support us
In whatever we will do
I will never leave you whatever path you want to take

I Am There!

Sunday, 8th September 2013 - Employers Hear Us Please?!

Well, I have had a busy week and a couple of foggy days in which I thought long and hard about this piece I have finished writing today apologies for the long wait, I hope it is worth it:-

Do you think you aren't good enough?

Do you have no faith to do something?

Why is this?

There are a lot of people who feel like this young and old, with or without mental health illnesses, I know I feel the same about me writing this piece and blog for those who have mental illnesses.

I am writing it not because, I know all about it - which I don't, but because I am experiencing, what you see with me is what you get, there are no cover ups all the pieces and poems I have written are through the good and the bad of my depression since April even since earlier than that.

My friends I know are experiencing the same thing, I asked them to contribute to my book, not just to make them feel good, but, to help others realise that people with mental illnesses can do things normal, they are human beings, like write a blog and a good one that 32,595 people can read over 5 months, I know that is not many, but, I want to shout out that we should be treated no differently to others, draw and help others understand mental health, there are many of us.

We have an illness that is hidden inside and that our past scars come out to darken it even more, our confidence has been shattered, we have low-self esteem, we feel lonely even with a lot of people around us, we want to be on our own, we feel paranoid, we lose interest in what we would usually do, we have a lack of sleep or too much sleep and for most of you who know these symptoms very well I could go on for a very long time.

First talking about these scars are hard for us, when we find someone to trust like I have it gets a little easier, but, even the hardest can be difficult to say to that one person. So for me writing them down is the easiest way which is why sometimes my blog can seem so personal, but, I want people to see it, because I don't want to hold it in any longer and I want to help others to come out and talk about their experiences that have helped the big black monster take them.

You will find in my posts and talking to different people the words or references to different names we use for our mental health illnesses, I call mine the big black monster, because the things that I have not got rid of from the past which it feeds on. The more I have tried to breakdown my pictures of the past the easier it has got.

So many times you get told you cannot change the past, I know that, you know that most of we know that it has led us to where we are now before I get told this. I know cynicism, you see I also know my past is helping me to be on my own two feet, to have a car, live eat and learn to I can be the better person I never was before, the independent thinking person.

I have learnt that I need to talk to others more about my past, school bullying, family, my ex-husbands and the fear I have always lived in of someone watching me by phone or looking at the things I do.

Learning to stand on my own two feet has been one massive change in my life, living without someone constantly controlling me. The monster soon crept up to me again and tapped into the memories I was trying to pack into the back of my mind and soon I was going down that road as the chemical imbalance became worse because I wouldn't do anything as I was trying to help someone else who was going through it all already, trying to stay strong, the more I stayed strong the more it was eating away at me as you will see from some of my older poems.

As I said before, I have learnt in the 6 months that talking through everything including my emotions have helped. I have been in and out of depression for the last 20 years or more and would so much to kick it in touch for me to be the one that controls my life not it, the only way I can do that is keep doing what I do now talk!

I express myself through my poetry and writing than I do through word of mouth. I have learnt this from others who tell me how much feeling they read in my writing, because I write as I think as someone think and talk.

Talking in the past 6 months even over the past year to friends, new friends and my best friends has been the best therapy, because they have let me talk about everything I needed to, I have also now found that my work is supporting me too.

My new manager and colleagues have the best theory in the world, which is my theory too, to talk about things whatever is makes a happy workplace, good to come to work, and helps you to concentrate on your work, so you are more productive. If you have a problem no matter how small or large you will work through it and talk through it. The team made me feel so welcome it feels like I have been there forever not just a couple of weeks.

I have been able to talk to them about a lot of things and they understand if I am quieter on an afternoon or a morning without thinking that I am just being moody, they will just check I am alright and if I don't need to talk, so you see it helps to have that someone anywhere to talk to and where I am in my life seems to be a good stage.

The team has also started to give me confidence in myself and a little bit of my self esteem back, which helps by giving me a little longer to work there and a manager who is always happy to help me get to the next step so a little encouragement from a few people can go a long way.

I only hope there are some employers who are listening to what I am writing today because this is what is needed and boy I can only tell you how much this has helped me to lift myself up.

Roger and his mum have seen such a difference in me, so much so that his mum has said to Roger how pleased she was to see the Old Susie back. There are still and will be times when I feel low, times which I need to handle and manage, probably because I am smashing pictures in my mind and putting the pieces that I want to see into my stained glass window, but, I can turn the mirror around and look at the inside and start to see a little bit more beauty.

We all need support from people, we are all fragile in our own ways, but, what we need are managers and a team that will talk to us normally with someone who is willing to go out of their way and talk to us, to ask us how we really are? Does it matter that all they will do is let it go over their heads of course it doesn't, it is to give us the strength to carry on through the day and help you help your team pull together, we need to end the stigma of Mental Health Illnesses.

We are people with a Mental Health Illness is hidden inside and until all this stigma ends we will keep going to work looking like we are in a bad mood, or going to the doctors to be signed off sick, all we are asking for to enable us to work is a support network or person to talk to so you can understand what we are going through.

We are not our illness, we have an illness, my illness is depression I have had it for over 20 years, yes my name is Susie Bell, I am 43 years old, I have supported and still support my partner Roger who is 44 through his depression, he in return also supports me as he is nearly at the end of his dark road. We're Ok

I write because it gives me pleasure, I write to help my feelings get out, I write to help kiss Mental Health Stigma to change

It really is #Timetotalk and #Timetochange!

Sunday, 8th September 2013 - Never Let Go of Shouting!!

Thank you so much for getting me through some of the darkest times of my depression, no this isn't the end, just a thank you for reading my posts and thoughts.

I have never been called Inspirational
I have never felt it
I always wanted to help people
Perhaps now is my time

I write purely from experience
I am not a trained psychologist or practitioner
It is all purely from my heart
And from my head

What you see is what you get
I will never change
Because I do not know how to be anything else
I don't shout a lot, just enough

I let the world turn around
But I want to make my stamp on it
A stamp with my size 7 feet
And chubby handed fist

I will shout with my writing
There will be such a big hole in the wall
I want to break down the walls for us
So that we can all go to work nomally

I want others to see us as people
With a mental illness hidden deep inside
Eating us up on the outside
That we need time and support to get through

We aren't like others
Are problems have unfolded as it has clouded our minds
We can work through it
But not always, we need help through those days

Some have help from home
Others need help from other places
We all need to say that we stand together

And never let go of shouting

Tuesday, 10th September 2013 –

The Path I have to and want to follow!

I have too many choices to make at the moment and I know what I want to do, but it feels like a junction or crossroads with too many signs saying if's and but's, please read on to see if you feel the same way at any time :-

I have come to another crossroads
A junction in my life
Or the start to a new career
As a stepping stone
My friends are here

As I get closer to how I think
The confusion and frustration
Of not knowing what to do is about me
The fog comes down
And blankets my brain

I think I know what to do
I know where I want to go
But unsure of the next steps to take
What words to write
How to get myself going

I want to move on
Start a new life
I have a new personal life
Now I want to move on in my work life
I have such encouragement

The people who are around me
Build my confidence day by day
Still I am unsure if I am good enough
Why can't I just accept this
Acceptance and trust go hand in hand

As I walk life's path
The sun starts to shine
Trying to shine through the fog
I know when I come to the crossroads
The decision will be the right one

The Path I have to and want to follow!

Tuesday, 10th September 2013 –

Thank you for helping me through!

It is in the US National Suicide Awareness Day today so I thought I would write a poem about my feelings on my low times for our fellow family with mental health illnesses and are feeling so low that it might inspire you to reach out to someone today and ask them how they are really feeling:-

I have been up and down this year
Along with many other years
I have had my real lows
Along with being normal or on a high
Most of all I am alive today

I have been thankful to be saved for today
For me to write to you
About how it is feeling at the very low end
How people saved me
By talking to me

I often asked why the angels left me
Why they let me be
I had to learn my lesson
A long and hard one
Of which I have learnt now

There are enough people who care
I have many things to do
The Angels saved me those few times
For something special
In my lifetime

My foggy mind is just clearing
To the crossroads I am at
The one way that I need to go
The crossroads has become straight
I know there will be bumps

The bumps I have overcome
There will be more along the way
I know though that being low
Was my worst time
I was lucky the last time to talk

The one lesson I have learnt
Is I am not alone
There are many of us around
Who have been there one time or another
And many more who are there now

If we know how you are feeling
We would reach out and hold you
Instead there are angels around you
Talk to a help line or two
It doesn't matter how many to help you through

You will be saved for another reason
Or may be the same one as me
But, never fear about living because we are here
Grasp each day as it comes and speak to a friend

Speak to someone to help you through

Thursday, 12th September 2013 –

Stop The Turning Of The World!!!

My Mind today has been quite foggy, light headed without knowing what is happening. :

Turn around and around and around
Stop, I want to get off
To stop the spinning
To know where I'm going

I am still stood at the junction
Turning around
Not a good place
Especially as it is ever so foggy

Work around
Up and down
See me for who I want to be
Where I want to go

Someone believe me
And hold my head
As it starts the whizzing
And you try to stop it

I wouldn't have thought
It was quite like this
The lowness I'm feeling
For no reason

I just want to sit and cry
Someone show me their hand
So that I can reach out
And feel like someone is holding out for me

I walk down the pathway
Back and forth
Not knowing where to go

Stop the turning of the World

Friday, 13th September 2013 - Live the Dream!!!

Hear what your past has to say to you, for some of us it may still be raw, but, for others they have let it pass over them, I want you to realise that thanks to your past you are here, you are meant to be here to achieve something and even if that is just living your life it is still an achievement some others wished that they could do and tell you to go on and live, achieve, let the fog lift away:-

Oh wow what a day
Round and round
Down and up
That is all it could be up

After the day like yesterday
I sat at my desk
Thinking about what I needed to get done
What was coming next

I wanted to realise my dream
The dream I have wanted
The one that I have started to achieve
Which was a life being happy

A life helping other people
Whichever way I turn
Go into work
I help people as well

Perhaps that is where my life is
Whatever I do
It is so I can help people
And do the best that I can

The problem is when I don't
That is when I feel low
When I have a very black day
The fog is lifting now

Someone told me to remember
What I have achieved
This year has been a year of achievement

And I hadn't realised
Until a friend reminded me
What I have done so far
I now know
I realise that I am not as hopeless

I can stand here at my crossroads
Ready to take the next junction
The one that will lead me on to the next path
The path that will help me

As I take that path
I know there will be many more
To cross
This is the one that will start me

The directions I have been in, in the past
Are what I think are the wrong ones
But actually they were right
Otherwise I wouldn't be here now

Learning what I am learning
Learning what I have already learnt
Thank you past
I may be trying to leave you behind

You were my life
I am my life
I will have my life

And my new achievements will be my new life

Sunday, 15th September 2013 –

Achievements & Dreams, Time To talk About Them

I don't think I have to explain too much about this one, just do it if not for me for yourself:

Achievements?

What do they have to do with getting myself out of this pitch black?

I have realised that achievements and dreams are important, they keep you going. Think about all the times you have done really good, the achievement. Think on those achievements.

Realising that dreams are as realistic as you make them. My one dream is that one day I will finally finish this depression or at least be able to manage it. The other dreams I have are to help end stigma with my writing, perhaps tv and my blog, they are not so extreme that it cannot happen.

Dreams are not always pie in the sky things that we sleep with, they are ideas that we build on, when we have achieved one step of them, then we build with it.

You see, I have been in and out of depressive episodes for over 20 years not knowing if I am ever going to come to the end or be able to hold on. I have tried to commit suicide three times with one only recently, I know that my dreams are to become real because why else would I have been saved it must have been for something, in fact I know it is.

I also know that I want this to become my dream to guide you to help yourself to shout about the mental health illnesses you have. To help you down a path of happiness not by forgetting the pains of the past, but, to make them easier.

Trying suicide made me realise how much I have in life, new friends, new love, new family and new supportive work colleagues. I couldn't have done this without the lessons of my past as well as my achievements of the past. I wouldn't be able to write about them either if I didn't have them.

What I am trying to say is that whatever has come from your past good or bad and achievement or a dream gone wrong it is what has made you today a strong, beautiful person and getting past it will only make you stronger and more beautiful. You can stand up strong, shout out your story or cower under the black cloud in the corner, if we don't say anything and keep quiet then we will never get past the brick wall that stands between us and our employers.

I have worked hard to get through all my depressive episodes and I would say this is probably the hardest period because I want to actually find a way to manage it or get rid of it for good. I have found someone who is willing to do whatever it takes to help me and support me through it.

Finding someone who understands about my depression and is able to talk things through with me no matter what has helped. I have been reaching out for the past 20 years with no help at all, I couldn't tell you if that would have changed me or not, I am just lucky enough to finally have found someone who knows what I have been through.
I have a few people supporting me one who told me to remember my achievements and that helped me to remember where I have been and what I have done, which is why I am saying to you. You have been strong for a very long time to get through everything and you are being strong by admitting that you need help, it is not a weakness.

Sharing with someone you trust is good for you, it helps to relieve when you are low and on the other side of it they will help to support you through the low times. They help you with the belief in yourself, the faith that you have deep down to achieve your dreams and to get out of the dark cloud that covers you at the moment. I know that if it wasn't for mine I wouldn't be here.

The strength, belief of what I will achieve in the future, my dreams for the future, with the love of Roger and support from other people including my new work team will help me get through it has boosted my confidence or I wouldn't believe in myself enough to publish my book next week on kindle.

The talking through my bad times has helped to break the pictures up and put them in such a way that I will be able to face them without tears to help someone else now. The mirror on the other side is starting to piece together, I will be able to look at both sides one day with a smile.

The talking at work about my depression has given me the strength to carry on with what I need to - my life. They have given me the confidence, by giving me trust and faith in myself again, something, I haven't had in a very long time. We all need it the talk at the beginning of the day to help push us through. Granted it didn't help me from stop wanting to kill myself on that Monday, but the one thing I will remember now is that I am not alone and there are enough people who care.

The wings of my angels surrounded me quickly that day to say that I will not be ending my life, I am to be kept for something better than ending my life early, that was when they tapped my partner on the shoulder and told him to look for me, so I had all my angels with me to comfort and help me through the worst day of the year and since then all I have done is build from it, talk to people including my counsellor and doctor.

I know what I am here for and that is to help you and other be able to talk about your mental health illnesses freely without feeling as though you are someone different, everyone is different we all wear a mask of some sort, we need to be able to lift those masks and be able to talk as they used to in years gone past, what we don't want them to do is to think we are nutters or crazy and the more we hide this the more we keep it inside, the more crazy people will think we are.

The more they will think that we do need locking away and keeping out of the community, we want to be treated as normal, because we are, we just have something inside that hurts, to them it may be strange to us it is an illness we need them to understand and hear what we are saying.

Hear what I am saying? Until we talk they won't listen or understand they will just roll in their own ignorance of what a mental illness is, will keep laughing, talking behind our backs and shouting names at us or saying we should be locked up..

The more we talk we help ourselves, the more we talk we help those who are around us to help those who will follow in our steps making their path way an easier one to recover or manage.

My journey has only just begun on the road to my recovery, it has not been an easy start with a lot of misunderstandings, silence and ignorance around me. I have now started on the road with more understandings, talking and support, this I would like for others not just for myself, I have been fortunate to find the right people to work with.

Talking is imperative to us to aid our recovery, to help with the support of all of us not just those with a mental illness or we would all struggle. Don't hide yourself away, ask for help you never know where you can find it.

Employers, all I ask for is you fi train your managers to talk to their employees, this makes a happy and productive workforce, believe me I know it, it has helped me so much and it has helped me to get through especially knowing that I am not so hopeless or worthless anymore. With my managers asking me if I am really okay, if there is nothing wrong when I am quiet instead of just leaving me alone and thinking I am just being moody, boy, having someone to talk about things has helped, it has eased my lowness as well at home and work.

My managers have given me such appreciation that I enjoy my work, not just worried about going to work and not being included, sitting on the outside of the team. I could talk about so much of having a supportive employer not just support outside of work. It is the best I have felt in a long time.

After 20 years the support I am receiving now will help to shake all of this and to be able to manage to realise that talking to anyone is the best therapy, no matter what way it is just say hello to someone today, no matter how sad they are and ask them how they really are, let them talk, if someone asks the same of you talk to them.

My name is Susie Bell, I am 42 years old, I am a writer, complaints assistant for the NHS, I have supported my partner Roger who is to turn 44 next Monday through his own mental health breakdown and is struggling to come to the end, with our love and support for each other we will both get through this including the support of friends around us and we have found a lot of them to talk to.

I think and know that this will tire you out, however I have to say it for those who are reading for the first time, #Timetotalk and #Timetochange

Sunday, 15th September 2013 - Becoming A Stronger Person

I want to help you and I want to tell you how I am getting through this with a little confidence and hope that things will help me:-

I have travelled a long, winding and bumpy road
To get where I am today
The new life I chose
To be myself
And change things for the better

Where my junctions have lay
And the stones have rolled
With the glass shattered behind me
I have looked back
But I am mainly looking forward

Looking forward to a bright future
Where my dull clouds part
And the only rain falls from the skies
Not my eyes or my heart
So here I stand to shout how I did it

I have sat still
I have moved around
I have struggled
I am still frustrated
And I still get upset

What I have done
Is talked
Written
Walked
And worked through most of it

I have held my head in my hands
I have tried killing myself
I have felt worthless and hopeless
I have been bullied by people

Now I stand tall, to say I am a stronger person for it all

Monday, 16th September 2013 –

The Only Way Is To Look Forward!

I have walked around in such a daze today, typical for a Monday:-

Round and round, Up and down
The world is spinning all too fast
So is time whizzing past
As the hours tick like minutes
And the minutes tick like seconds
Where does it go?

Back and forth, fly high and fly low
The planes and the trains
The cars and the bikes
With the people walking by
Until they look like ants
How does it all happen?

Bright colours and dull colours, with a rainbow up above
Created by the sun
And a rainstorm passing through
The clouds are dull and then they brighten
Which helps to lift the gloom
Why should it happen?

Zip and zap, slow and fast
My mind cannot cope with such a slope
I wish things could stay still for a while
No change or pain, no hurt just gain
With the dullness turning to light
When will this happen?

Look left now look right, look up and look down
Don't look back just in front, only forwards
This is the way that you will go
The same way as I, because we have no other
What is in front is our new life and a way to talk

We will make friends along the way, that is how.

Tuesday, 17th September 2013 - Talk To End The Stigma!!

If we don't talk it won't end, If we stand behind our doors, they will not open, reach out and hold someone's hand, talk to them and ask for help it all starts with you, you are stronger than you believe, you have got this far to admit you have an illness, go one step further and seek the help you need, there is nothing wrong with it, in fact you are the better and stronger person for it, go on talk and end the stigma:-

I spoke to a stranger today
Something I don't often do
I opened up
And the rain fell down
Not just outside, but from my eyes

The pain opened up
And the hurt came flooding out
The numbness began
The wall which I wanted to hide behind
You know the one where you are unsure why

Why? You ask
Why now
Why today
How can I do this
You know that it will make things better

My life has been full of triggers
For every time I turned around
Something else was triggered
Now I am triggered by pain
The thoughts of what have happened in the past

Thoughts of wanting to move forward
To cower away from all of this anguish
Somewhere, I know though
This is going forward
Talking to someone who can help me

The first person who has to give help
Is you
You have to step outside

Reach out to someone
Hold their hand and talk

Reaching out is the most amazing thing
It is so empowering
It is such a lift to you
It won't be an automatic cure
It is the step on the right road

Talk today
Change something no matter how small
Walk with someone
Have a coffee
Take a minute from your dark place

Unless we talk about it we won't end the stigma!!

Wednesday, 18th September 2013 –

Let the light in to brighten your cloud

My day has been busy and my evening will get even busier as I prepare my book from my blog for Sunday's deadline of publishing on kindle, but, never too busy for me to write a poem for my readers who either enjoy, feel inspired or can empathise with my feelings for the day:-

Busy Busy Busy bee
Where does the time go
Nobody knows
Today has flown as quick
As the bee buzzed by

This days have gone quick
Towards my upcoming holiday
The one thing I am looking forward to
I know I have much more to with that
I continue working afterwards as well

What you have to do is think about the future
The past is behind you
It doesn't mean it won't hurt
You work forwards
And don't stand still

Working forwards
With talking to others
One step at a time
Helps you to move on
One day you will only look on

You won't have to look back
Because all of what you have behind
Will have helped you towards you moving on
You may not feel it now
But, believe me it will hurt, will only make you stronger

The more you move forwards
The stronger you become
The stronger you become
The quicker and less painful the past will get
What you don't want to do is stop for too long

Move on slowly with each step you take
It is alright to step back as well
Aslong as you can see the step forward
The dream will be there one day
For you to build on

The achievements you want to make
Remember all the achievements you have made
The steps you take towards these
Will be good steps
The steps forward that will be less painful

Walk forward
Walk Tall
Feel strong
Talk high

Let the light in the sky brighten your cloud.

Thursday, 19th September 2013 –

When I have reached the top!

Even though there are some exciting and new things in my life and future, there are still some darkening thoughts about what to do next and why do I feel so flat about them. Don't give in, because I certainly won't as people keep telling me one step at a time and that is slowly does it:-

I seem to be following a light
The smallest of holes in my big dark cloud
Perhaps a ray of light
That will help me
Down the pathway to where my life will be

As I hear the music coming with the light
I can feel my feet tapping along the path
A dance that only I can learn
If I am willing to ask for the help
Help from people who are willing to teach me

As I try to hear the instructions
Sometimes they seem a bit muffled
And I don't understand
Even though I keep asking the questions
I wonder if I am ever going to get around

Of course I am
I am made of stronger stuff than that
But, I also know it takes a lot of hard work
To have so much faith in myself
When others already do

To feel the confidence of others
Glowing inside me is great
Until I sit on my own
I think about the leap of faith and trust they have
And ask my can't I see it in myself

You have it in you
I can only see the past
I have to think of tomorrow
Not yesterday
Or the pain that loses all my self-esteem

You are beautiful
In fact you are gorgeous
And amazing
That is what you tell me
One day I will see all this

When I have reached the top!

Thursday, 19th September 2013 - In A Room Of People

I have a friend who is feeling as we are and will still say she is fine, because she thinks that what we have is a weakness and not a strength, see what I say in my poem:

How lonely can you feel
Standing in a crowd or room of people
It is lonely
When all you can hear is chattering

Watch their lips moving
You turn around
Look at all their faces
How can it feel lonely

The silence around you
Inside your head
Is so deafening
What do you do instead

As you take a step
To the right
And one to the left
Boy I might aswell be on my own tonight

What a feeling of bewilderment
To fear a crowd of people
All because you feel lonely

In a room of people

Friday, 20th September 2013 –

A step back for me, but a step forward for you

This from a good day to a bad day and I am sorry to say goodbye to so many people, who have supported and helped me through everything -

It is sad when you lose work colleagues
As you move from office to office
Even sadder when you lose friends
Because you overwhelm people
I only want to be heard

I feel sad tonight and worthless
Because I feel my work is no good
What I am trying to do is obviously stupid
Why am I doing this book
Why am I writing this blog

There is nothing wrong with me
Because I have been working
I have been writing
Never mind the five weeks off during the summer
Because I was poorly and feeling low

II have nothing wrong with me
Let me feel the pain of being rejected
Just when I think that everything is right
Not everything is though is it
Am I that much of a door mat

I have worked so hard to be who I am
And now I feel it all crumbling down around me
That a few people cannot accept me
I have tried to make steps
Now I am going back again

I feel very low
And as though nobody wants to hear me
Unless I am feeling this low
Nobody wants to hear the positives

Just the negatives
That is where I am today
Sat here crying
Because someone has made me feel offensive
I can't keep up the pretence anymore
Just break down in tears

When I am well enough
I will be strong enough to accept these things
At the moment
I am just low
Thank you all for your support

Saturday, 21st September 2013 –

One small step upwards every day

Looking forward instead of sitting around for too long, I have written a poem about being able to take that step back and out :-

One more step along the world I go
Is there any chance of taking a step back
Things have changed for me
So quickly and so much lately

Of course I can
What I must keep an eye on is
What my next step will be
When I take a step back

I can rest
Relax
Take it easy
Then brush myself down

The next step I will take
Will be the one towards the light
The one across the junction
Is it too big, of course not

That's fine
Just allow me to rest
Give me time
To make that next step

It won't take long
Too long
I maybe back on my feet tomorrow
Tomorrow is a new day with a new way

One small step upwards every day

Sunday, 22nd September 2013 –

You Dream to Achieve..Isn't it Time?

Where I would like to start is achieving from building your dreams step by step, you can do it if you want to change things:-

Have you ever dreamed a dream that has nearly come true?

Have you ever wanted to build on the dream you have seen?

Have you ever thought that the dream you have will ever be an achievement?

I have to all three of those, if I could tell you how hard it is to build on the dream you are so passionate about, the one thing you truly want to achieve and believe in yourself which is difficult especially the way you are feeling at the moment.

Don't you dare say it, don't tell me to 'snap out of it' that only sends me the opposite way. I need encouragement, to take each step slowly and carefully to realise that I can achieve this, achieve What I have thought would be unachievable, in fact I got encouraged by Roger to take each step carefully and with his help I have been able to achieve and get my story out.

My dream is that the whole world would understand all mental health illnesses, alas one step at a time, the next dream is let people know they are not alone, again though one step at a time, the other is to help all mental illness sufferers be able to work if they can by helping employers understand and end the workplace stigma, again I am going to get told one step, so here I am doing the one step….

One step at a time and you can achieve your dreams, I have over the past twenty years suffered from depression and sticking out like a sore thumb, the edge of a team, the odd one out from my friends, just alone in the crowd.

My dream is that I can shout loud enough to be heard by others who do not understand what a mental health illness is, someone who thinks they are absolutely perfect and would never believe that a mental illness would happen to them, it can and you never know it might.

1 in 4 people suffer from a mental health illness, I am one of them, you could be next and it would be even worse if you want to play ignorance to that, I hope it doesn't happen, I hope nothing like this ever touches you, half my life has been spent fighting this horrible

illness, one I have never yet learned how to manage, I will with the thoughts of my dreams in front of me.

For those of you who already have a mental illness, your dreams will keep you moving down the new path, listening to the new music of your future with the new dance you are going to learn, to put together the picture of your past so that you can look at it and say thank you for where you are today.

I said this to my counsellor, I am still unsure how he took this. If my past hadn't happened to me and I didn't have depression then where would I be now. I thank my past for realising that I could write and that I have depression. As much as I hate it, it has given me the passion to live and fight for something, fight for mental health illnesses. I wouldn't have stood by Roger through his illness and he wouldn't be standing by me with his friends and mine.

You see I am building on my dream by writing my blog and by writing my pieces to tell the World about how we should help, not get special treatment, get a little help from anyone around us.

I would like people not to sound shocked when I tell them I have depression, because they tell me that I work so well or look okay, the person behind the smile they do not know, they would find out if only they would read my book.

I wrote poems before April and wondered how I could use them to talk to people, to reach out, I decided to build a blog, then I bought a .com website www.heartilymindful.com and built on the website even more the next step to my achievement, when I finally got to 30,000 readers of my blog I suddenly realised how I was touching people from around the world with my words, one more step of my dreams achieved.

The one last step that happened was compiling a book from this blog, this would go back and forth shall I/shallnot I and Roger kept encouraging me and he said I have started this compilation and we will finish it, so, it happened I got 3 people to review the first 3 months of my blog and Sara Breidenstien of Kissing Stigma Goodbye Facebook page to do my preface, Roger to do an epilogue for me.

Last night, after all my hard work, Roger's and Sara's I finished my book, I hit the publishing button and sent my dream to one of the biggest, bravest and most courageous achievements I had done in my life, I stepped out into the big wide world, to tell other sufferers that I feel the same as they do and that they are NOT alone, there is someone else as they are day in day out struggling.

There is nothing great about writing, I am just not good at speaking, so I am building my dreams on this so I can achieve, end MH Stigmatism, MH Sufferers you are not alone, talk about my story and be brave with it, accepting me for me, being able to help those who are in a place of work and having a hard time, talking to employers, helping those who are ignorant to MH to understand.

My name is Susie Bell, I am 42 years old, a sufferer of depression, author of **Heartily Yours**, Blog writer of www.heartilymindful.com, if you have anything to say, say it to me and let me answer you, I am stronger for what I have done.

My Partner is Roger Parker, he will be 44 years old tomorrow, he has had a mental breakdown, he has helped me edit and compile **Heartily Yours**, he helps me with research, he supports me and encourages me as I have with him through my Mental Illness.

I would like to thank you for helping me to build on my dream and my dreams can only get bigger and better now parts of them have been achieved. Please take a look at my book **Heartily Yours by Susie Bell** on kindle, Thank you today for reading and sharing my piece and hearing what I write. Dreams are hard to follow, but, you can do it, you have to talk and to change in order to do it, they will change as your path changes, each step comes closer to where you are meant to be and what you are meant to achieve.

Thursday, 26th September 2013 - A Bright New Future!!

Take a look at how I have felt over the last four days :-

Wow, what a brill few days I have had
No writing
No thinking
Lots of loving
Lots of drinking

The time has flown by
And wind driven right through my hair
Sea at my ankles
Sand beneath my feet
Sun blowing the clouds away up above

I have had my time of loneliness
In a crowd of four
Where I have felt
Like I am sitting on the fence
Soon joined back in again

Why can't I feel something
I still feel the numbness
The feeling that I should be happy
All of the time
I have come a long way to before

I am sitting here thinking now
About the photos I have taken
And the poems written in my head
The darkness has come over me
Even from day to day

My smile is seen hiding the pain
Where I have been before
The past hurt, trying to paste over
With the new memories of the future
Ones I have created on this holiday.

As we pack up to go home
I will remember the good times in this holiday
The times I have been happy
Because this is my new future
Not my past.

If I were to tell you I will work on
The time I have just had
Which is giving me new memories instead of the past
I have smashed some pictures
I am now able to place them into my frame

Step by step
Road by road
Path by path
Junction by Junction

I am making my way to my bright future!

Friday, 27th September 2013 –

End the silence of Mental Health!!

I have learnt a lot over the last few days of my holiday, that the footsteps in my poem are not just of mine but others who are reading my posts and those who believe I can make it through all of this, there is one thing though I will promise, my posts will not end until such time as the silence is broken! -

See those footprints
The ones that just have one trail
Now I have two
Not even just two sets
Several with a set of wings

The set of wings have been wrapped around
The one set of steps were my own
Then the second is my partners
As I have seen over the past year I have seen
Others slowly over time passing have joined mine

Knowing that I could talk out
To others has helped so much
Realising that it I have nothing to be ashamed of
To think that someone wants to help me
To get somewhere, where I have never been

Whilst helping myself, helping others
So those who have joined me
Have been helped as well
Holding my head up high
Straightening my back and stepping out with courage

The courage and strength in my heart
That has never been there before
To let my fear hold me back
Until now I have finally found the voice to speak out
For myself and for others

Come with me
Step forward
Making a set of footsteps with me
Allow another brick to come out of that wall
The wall that is called stigma

This stigma is our silence
We are not wanting attention
We are wanting help to come out
And find ourselves inside and out
Take a good look inside

Take the time to change
To talk
To walk with others
To walk and talk with me
Let me hold your hand and lead you somewhere you want to go

End the silence of Mental Health!!

Saturday, 28th September 2013 –

We Will Walk and Talk Together! (Not a poem)

As you can see a lot of my holiday has been quite reflective over the past year, I have smashed a few memories and made new ones, ones that are part of the life I have created for myself again. You don't need to know how much , but, I have gone through enough over the past years to realise why I am where I am and why it has taken longer this than any other time to come through:-

How do you know that you can't go any further?

That where you are is all you are ever going to be?

Have you stepped out of the zone you have been in for so long?

If you think I have never had any thoughts as the above you are so heartily wrong, because I have, I had them for many, many years and I still have them, I still go back to the thoughts of never doing anymore than I have because, others have drummed this into me, I never reach out enough, I am never going to be intelligent enough.....

You can believe what you want and stay where you are if you want to. You can dream of a pot of gold that you will never reach at the end of that rainbow, it will only ever be a dream if you don't even take one step outside of the zone you have been in forever and you can stay there, I will tell you something until you make one move towards a change your zone will always be the same one.

Over my lifetime I have had to change so much and not always for the better. You will now say but look where you are now, I know where I am now, I know what has happened to me, if it wasn't for what had happened in my past I wouldn't be sat here talking to you and talking about what happened to help me.

I sat under the cloud or with the big black monster raging inside me for far too long, because others said they had understood what I was going through, leaving me to get better on my own, yet I never really came out of it.

It started when I was about 20 if not before then, what I could never get past was why? How I was ever going to get out of it, I thought it was me so I drifted from relationship to relationship, job to job with no real control over my life because it was others that had the remote and knew exactly which buttons to press to my heart, I couldn't hear anyone outside this because the cloud was still over my ears blocking my hearing, my lesson was learnt a couple of years ago.

What I have found is that I was the only one that had to help myself to change things, I was going to stay in the same thing every time if I never got out of it, the lock was there and accessible I just had to find a key and I did that with three friends, between the four of us we unlocked my new future and I found that I was more than friends with one of these and that is where I am now. You see I had to take a step outside of that zone to change where I was.

The new man in my life was allowing me to be me even though we were both going down the same road or up the same hill whichever you want to say, I slowed down as much as I could to allow Roger to go through his breakdown, you wouldn't believe how hard this is to keep an illness from someone you love so much, he didn't realise that I was ill until a couple of months later and started to see the change in me. I told him a few months later, I sat on the edge of our bed and told him I knew exactly where I was and he said I know, I told him that I had felt it for a very long time as the tears flowed down my face and he held me tight, the first thing he said as I had said to him was to go to the doctor and a week or two later I did.

You see, I had stepped so far out of my zone, but, I needed to make the changes in the past year to get to where I was, that was when I started writing more, more so poetry, it helped me to get out what was inside.

Easter Bank holiday weekend I started my blog - Heartily Mindful, I said to Roger, perhaps someone may read my posts, so that is what I have done and step by step, I have got more and more people, I got nervous, because again this was stepping outside of another zone, into somewhere I have never been, with help from Roger, I finally got the blog up and running after three months wrote my book on the first three months just published last weekend on Kindle and in paperbook on Amazon around the world - Heartily Yours by Susie Bell, take a look at it and see what you think, perhaps buy it as 50p goes to mind for every book. The next will be an American Mental Health Organisation and different countries for each quarter.

This helped me to get through many things including each day, knowing that I would be coming home to be able to tell my feelings, it helped me to understand what my day had been like and when I read back I can see what I was like, how mental health can change you bit by bit. There have been months where I have been some dark times.

I soon found groups and pages I could share my blog with and found I wasn't alone in this, that as well as mine and Roger's footsteps in the sand there were others joining me, people who were supporting me or inspiring me to keep moving along my new pathway, I could tell you a few of those, Sara Breidenstein - Kissing Stigma Goodbye, I'm OK -

facebook page, Dominic Stenning - @patient_leader, twitter, Elefriends forum - Mind, If it hadn't been for some of these and Roger I would never have been where I am.

I was saved by and Elefriends on a bank holiday Monday not too far back this year, because of a bully or altercation with an extended family member. I believe of all the times that I have been saved from taking my own life, I was saved for a reason, to keep going with what I am doing, I am still not sure what that great person has in mind for me yet, I know that I will keep encouraging others to talk, to change, inspiring them, helping them to understand that they aren't alone in any of this, there is someone else out there to help them.

One day we will be able to talk about our mental illnesses openly without the shame that surrounds it now, we shouldn't keep quiet, the more we do this the more we will be kept in the dark and shame surrounding us. Stand up with me, take my hand, walk with me towards the wall of stigma in front of us and we will talk it or even shout it down in whichever way we can.

I will stand up for this in whatever way I can and will because this is important, it is an illness that cannot be measured or seen it is hidden inside of you and me, some of us will recover fully and then there are some of us who will not!

I walk along a beach with many footsteps on it joining me at every angle and I know there will be many more, hopefully employers, as well as sufferers and advocates for ending mental health stigma. The sea will lap at my feet and wash away some prints, they are prints that I will not worry about because they are not strong enough to stand up, they will join me again and more will join us nearer to the future the group of steps will get bigger and then the wind will be behind us helping us on our way.

Stand up with me, walk with me and we will all stand up together for the end of Mental Health Stigma.

My name is Susie Bell, Author of Heartily Yours, Mental Health Sufferer at the age of 42 for over twenty years. My partner is Roger Parker, he is 44 years old and is near the end of his recovery from his breakdown, now my main supporter.

Stand together, stand united, we will walk and talk together!

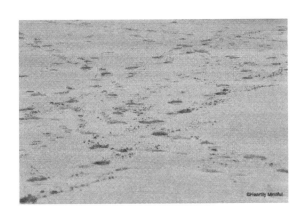

Saturday, 28th September 2013 - Thank you for being there!

Take a look at the poem I don't think I need to say too much to it :-

Somewhere Over the Rainbow
Is what I heard Israel singing one day
Along with what a Wonderful World
Little did I know that I would ever be able to sing it
To anyone

I can sing it to you
Because at the moment
This is where I am with you
Somewhere Over the Rainbow
And you have created such a Wonderful World

Every day we take each step at a time
We walk hand in hand
Along the white beaches he sings about
As we did on Wednesday morning
What a time we have had and we will carry on

Each time we walk
We talk with each other to make our lives easier
So we can both get past
Things that have caused our pain
The pain that is slowly going with new memories

Each time we walk
Walk with each others footsteps
Holding each others hands
It is walking away from the times
Times we can say thank you for where we are today

I know you think I am mad
Just think about the chain of events
We have walked in parallel lives
We have nearly met four times
Now destiny has brought us together where we are now

I thank you for my past and the people in it
If I didn't have it I wouldn't be talking to you now
I wouldn't be able to help you become stronger
To help your tears stop falling
Realising that you are not on your own.

You are never alone
You will always be able to turn to me
The strength you have inside
Has carried me through
The support I have needed and still need

We will be there for each other no matter what
Just remember what Izzy sings
And we will get by everything
This is my moment and I will be free
That is what I remember what you have done for me

I am doing what I have to and I will carry on
Thank you for being there!

Sunday, 29th September 2013 - It Has To Stop!! (Not a Poem)

When I stand on my own two feet, I will not stop writing to end discrimination or others ending their lives because we won't talk!! It has to stop! :-

My feet have walked a thousand miles if not more and they will walk a few million yet through the years that I have left, this may not have happened if it wasn't for the fact that I may not be sat here writing this piece.

There were several times my life could have ended if I hadn't been stopped, the first time was twenty years ago a night I could look back on with dread, but, thinking what happened, knowing that if my friend and I had not made a pact to phone each other if either of us wanted to end our lives, I sat writing a letter as I made this phone call and doing what I thought I was helping me to leave this world, when my friend couldn't speak to me she called my parents and an ambulance, at the time I didn't think about calling anyone else not even the Samaritans, the things that are now in place for help is so much better, so much more accessible than they were back then.

To be able to talk to someone was so much harder, the counsellor I had back then didn't believe I needed counselling just to go home and sort things out with my "husband" what husband the one who worked every hour he could and one who would go straight into work as soon as we finished our holiday, spent half the holiday worrying about what was going on at work. I probably didn't really know what the problem was back then, but, that was what talking was about talking through things to help me understand and try to put them right.

I was saved by my friend, an angel or my parents if you want for a reason, perhaps I have walked a lot of mileage going back and forth along this road, made so many tracks in my own beach, stood looking out to sea wondering where to go crying a river that made that sea crash against the rocks wishing at times to be swallowed up, I am here, to be able to tell you that things change for a reason, but as I have said many times you have to be that one person to take that footstep, make the one footstep onto a clean part of the beach of life in order to make that change.

Over the years I have thought I make that change, but, feel like I am still stuck at that same place until now.

Yes, I have tried to end my life again since then, thanks for fireman and my angels I was saved to be able to tell you this story and only just recently when I should have known better and talked to the Samaritans, but I wasn't thinking that way instead I harmed myself and hurt others like Roger. I felt hopeless enough because I was not tough enough to stand up against a bully in my own home even after I told them to stop shouting at me.

The Samaritans and many other organisations in the UK do a fantastic job of trying to help yourself and myself if we need help. I have emailed them in the past if I needed help when I couldn't talk about things to anyone except Julie and she wasn't free to talk to so I would write it in an email.

When I met Roger last Summer over a year ago, little did I know what was going to happen and that he was going to be the one human angel I was going to have to lean on and support, little did either of us know that he would need my support until he got there a couple of months later, you now ask me how did I know he was the one and he was going to be different to the others?

I didn't I was worried and so insecure throughout his breakdown that he would drop me or not want me when he came out the other side, in fact nothing is further from the truth, since we have both talked, we have both talked about things more easily and more freely than with any of the other partners we have been with. He knows me so well.

He is my soulmate, my bestfriend, the only one I will talk to about everything, we don't argue, we discuss and compromise, which I have never had, I don't have to fight old ghosts and he doesn't with mine. Slowly, but, surely as friends we have grown stronger as a couple, I never have to ask about him leaving me, I have no insecurities with him anymore.

He has helped me to work through some of my past, we will work through a lot more, he gives me the encouragement and supports me when it is needed a friend rather than a lover, which I have never had before, he came to the doctors once to make sure that I was telling them everything and to help keep me calm.

You need to reach out to someone in your life, a friend, someone you work with, family it doesn't matter, someone who understands or will understand and will learn along the road with you. It sometimes isn't what they say it is them being there to listen and hear what you are saying. This is why I think employers should have this and not make those like us with mental health illnesses feel as though we should hide away and feel ashamed about what we have.

Not, to let us feel like we should hide in a corner or be locked away with key thrown away, I have worked a through with it, now I have understanding managers. Previously I didn't say anything as I heard people laughing at someone who took tablets for this, I was in counselling, but the counselling never came quick enough, the access to it didn't help me with this job and I realised that I was unable to carry on with the position and it wasn't right for me, it was the strongest thing I ever did the admittance that I was unable to carry on, which my manager and myself agreed on after a discussion with Roger the night before.

I then found a position which took me a few days to realise that I could talk about this and I am still there with my managers giving me the encouragement, support and help with confidence that nobody except Roger has given me in a very long time.

Twenty years on I am sat here writing this story of me to you because I do not want you to feel alone in the tears that you shed, the cloud and the monster inside your head, the emotions that can affect every step of your life and whatever way you go, it is to help you, to tell you that YOU can do this, you can get through this!

Take a look around you, And I mean stop and see what you would want to do, how you would want to change about what is around you and take a step outside of your comfort zone, or you will just keep going as you are now, just one small step towards something that will change. In order to change we are the ones who have to take the step we can ask for help how, but, we have to do it, even if it is talking about it or even talking to someone.

Today, take that one step, make that difference in your life, I know I am making it sound easy, but, believe me I know that it isn't, it has taken a lot of confidence to stand up and say all of this, I have been where you are.

Slow those tears from falling, slow the waves crashing against the rocks let the sea calm down and step forward to feel the temperature the one step you need to make.

My name is Susie Bell, I am 42 years old, Authoress of Heartily Yours and sufferer of severe depression for over 20 years. My Partner is Roger Parker, 44 years old, recovering from a mental breakdown, we both stand together to support each other and to support the ending of Mental Health Stigma - discrimination.

One day we will get better because now is the #timetotalk and #timetochange

Epilogue

Well, thank you, for reading my book, the second in the series of Heartily Yours from my Heartily Mindful Blog

I have walked a thousand miles and written a million words, I would like to continue writing them so that others are able to understand why we should let mental health me known and not just be hidden.

We talk the talk, but, can we walk the walk. That is why I do it and all in my own name there is no fake name for me to write these experiences under, they have all happened sitting on the fence looking inside a team instead of sitting within a team, being part of a team. Sit on an evening watching the doors slam in my face and feeling alone oh so very alone, because nobody would talk about anything and not enjoying the evening.

My contract ended with one employer early because I couldn't do the work, because I realised that I was unable to stay at the company, everything was done amicably thankfully, I moved on to what I am doing now where mindfulness is found a lot in the NHS, where accepting someone for who or what they have gone through is enough and is helpful for them. They will know when I can say no to something.

For the last part of this book it is where I can say thank you and such a big thank you to Barbara, Paul and Julie for helping me pull through this, to help me relax, accepting me for me and that not every team leave you out, realising that there are others in the same position.

For Managers to talk to you on the same level, encouraging me every step of the way to go on to things a little further on, for what they have done to teach me that what I have been through helps me in the work that I do. To push me with a gentle push on the back, to push you to the light where you change to you.

How have I found time to work and write? Because it is the one thing that has kept me going, there were times when I haven't written and when I couldn't because all I wanted to do was cry.

Knowing it is nearly time to publish is when I know that it is time to keep writing. The comment I put at the front of the book was one made just before I went on holiday, I wouldn't and couldn't stop crying that night. I have told you that I have been saved three times for a reason, if you can't see it then neither can I but, I am still here, the comment that was made if that is the only person I help, I would be pleased I have helped save someone from losing their life and harming themselves. To that anonymous person and comment I will say thank you.

Now I would like to end this note by saying please take the time to see what some of the facebook pages or blogs have to be able to help you or to help understand and thank you for reading my book.

List of Mental Health Organisations

UK

Mind
Website: www.mind.org.uk
Info line : 0300 123 3393
Email: contact@mind.org.uk

Time To Change
Led by Mind & Rethink Mental Illness
Website: www.time-to-change.org.uk
Email: info@time-to-change.org.uk

Rethink Mental Illness
Website: www.rethink.org
Info line : 0300 5000 927
Email   : advice@rethink.org or info@rethink.org

SANE
Website: www.sane.org.uk
Helpline: 0845 767 8000
Email   : From their website

USA

Mental Health America
Website:www.mentalhealthamerica.net
Helpline: 1-800-273-TALK(8255) - USA dial
Email   : info@mentalhealthamerica.net

American Foundation For Suicide Prevention
Website: www.afsp.org
Helpline: 1-800-273-TALK (8255)
Email: info@afsp.org

Australia

Mental Health Association Australia
Website: www.mentalhealth.org.au
Helpline : 1300 729 686 - Australia dial
Email   : info@mentalhealth.org.au

Canada

Canadian Mental Health Association
Website: http://www.cmha.ca/
Helpline: Please find in your own Provence on www.cmha.ca/get-involved/find-your-cmha
Email   : Please find in your own Provence on www.cmha.ca/get-involved/find-your-cmha

Centre for Suicide Prevention
Website: suicideinfo.ca
Several different email and telephone numbers as in different areas across Canada.

Some of the above organisations have their own forums. 50 pence for every book sold is being donated to Suicide Prevention in the United States as they it is a very good forum for those with Mental Health Illnesses.

Facebook Pages

Kissing Stigma Goodbye
Im OK
Mental Illness Is Hidden
Heartily Mindful
Footsteps to Mental Health
I am Not My Illness

There are a lot more that are community mental health pages who are not medical staff, however their experience as you have heard from Sara Breidenstein in the Preface of my last book, please look on them as there is a wide range of different pages, if I went on to talk about them we would be in a few months when my next book would be due.

Printed in Great Britain
by Amazon

29964686R00121